MY WAY WIRELESS SPY, THEN DOCTOR

PAUL MOFFITT

BALBOA.
PRESS

A DIVISION OF HAY HOUSE

Balboa Press books may be ordered through booksellers or by contacting:

Balboa Press
A Division of Hay House
1663 Liberty Drive
Bloomington, IN 47403
www.balboapress.com.au
1 (877) 407-4847

Print information available on the last page.

ISBN: 978-1-5043-1538-8 (sc)
ISBN: 978-1-5043-1539-5 (e)

Balboa Press rev. date: 11/09/2018

Contents

Reader Comments... ix

Preface xi

Medicine Must Wait 1

The Sea Is a Dangerous Place 13

A Doctor at Last.. 20

Just Another Day in General Practice.................................... 22
- Mr Slipped Disc 23
- The Things We Do 26
- Re-Bore 29
- Husbands Beware 31
- Tommy Calendar and the Giant................................. 32
- Postscript 33

Come Urgently, Doctor.. 34
- Crying Wolf 34
- Threatened.. 35
- A Gaping Hole 37
- Call Me "Master" 39
- Addendum.. 43

Poisoning with Intent... 45
- Aunty Thally 45
- The Fisher Family 49
- Stanley Jones 51
- Mr X 52

Poisoning by Accident 55
- Deadly Cough Drops 55
- Black Licorice—Too Much of a Good Thing....................... 57
- Quinine with Metoprolol... 58

In the Ring 60
- Brian Sams: The Fighting Coal Miner 61
- Lionel Rose: Sweat and Tears 64
- Pat Rafter: More Sweat 69
- Al Burke: Wrong Diagnosis 70
- Allan Williams: The Quiet Performer 72
- OTHER CHAMPIONS 75

Leaving Cessnock.. 77
- The Sense of Smell 77
- The London Years.. 82
  o Everyone Needs a Friend 82
  o Saved by Being Learned Proper 86

Doctor at Sea 89

Up There for Thinking 94
- Fooling the Taxman 94
- Just a Little Way Now... 97

The Basics of Diagnosis 103
- Palpation 105
- Percussion 108
- Auscultation 111
- Your Role Is Important 114

Making Ward Rounds 118
- Imposters... 118
- Psittacosis 126
- Charcot's Foot 129

Contributing to Medicare: The Pros and Cons....................131

The Doctor and the Law 135

No Laughing Matter... 139

What Happened, Doc?.. 144

Ben, Vince, and a Thing Called Superfoetation 149

The Beginnings of Diabetes Education...............................153

Some Wry Observations...170

    •   Conversation with Jodie.......................................170

    •   Addendum..171

    •   Aural–Oral Synchronisation Syndrome 172

    •   The Pendulum 173

    •   Commonsense 174

    •   Moffitt's Foxhole Test 176

Reader Comments

It is the best book that I have ever read including textbooks and so informative. I could not put it down. *Dr Joe Davis, ophthalmologist (personal communication)*

I can honestly say that this book (apart from the Bible) is the best. *Bernadette Barry, New Zealand*

I learnt something useful in THE SENSE OF SMELL... about how ladies tend to not be able to smell their own perfume after it has been on awhile ... and I thought it wasn't working properly!!

You know, the thing that keeps coming through to me from reading this book is your own massive personal knowledge, both practical and theoretical, your keen observation, your sense of humour and of the ridiculous, and your ability to place events in a time that we "older generation" can recognise and appreciate. *Dale Bailey, schoolteacher/grazier*

How very kind of you to send me a copy of *My Way*. I have already started reading it and am enjoying your fresh style and ready wit immensely. Congratulations.

I so much agree with you about good history and physical examination. I often preach the same lesson myself.

Congratulations on excellent work. *Professor Sir Gustav Nossal, Australian of the Year 2000 (personal communication)*

I really loved all the stories from your young days in the army (what a valuable AWOL that was for the navy) through the great yarns of GP in Cessnock and later through your specialty years and ending with your massive contribution to the management of diabetes. Your obvious enjoyment and satisfaction in your work is shared by many of us, not least of all me, and it was a delight as a reader to share your pleasure in sound diagnosis based upon clinical findings while at the same time mourn its diminishing emphasis with the rise and rise of technology. Your patient's answer to "when did your budgie die?" had me laughing out loud. *Dr Kim Ostinga, orthopaedic surgeon (personal communication)*

I have read your book *My Way* from cover to cover with huge enjoyment and admiration! I think it gives those who never had the privilege and pleasure of having known you some insight into your unique character and style. Your clinical acumen, honed carefully in Cessnock, London and then Royal Newcastle Hospital, really shines through in these fabulous stories. etc. *Professor Pat McGorry, Australian of the Year 2010 (personal communication)*

In 1977 I came to Newcastle as Professor of Medicine and met Paul Moffitt, who had transformed the way that patients were treated, making them Individuals. This was by forming Diabetic Education Centres that spread throughout the world. His unique and engaging style of communication has resulted in an exciting collection of stories about life as a young doctor in the mining towns of the Hunter. Stories that make you realize how much you can gain by listening to your patients. *Professor Trefor Morgan, Foundation Professor of Medicine, University of Newcastle (personal communication)*

Preface

Good fortune has introduced me to many unusual people and situations during and prior to my sixty-three years of medical practice. (I started practice in 1953 and ceased full-time practice in 2003, at age seventy-eight, but I remained a registered medical practitioner, treating friends and former patients for free, until 2015.) My experiences throughout a long life have ranged from fascinating to frightening, and I wish to share some of them with you.

I begin these reminiscences by describing my more than three years as an Australian soldier intercepting Japanese wireless messages during World War II and my wonderment at how a fake *Akagi*, impersonating the real aircraft carrier *Akagi* prior to its attack on Pearl Harbor, could have deceived US wireless interceptors. I write of these events of seventy years ago because they may be interesting and informative, but also because most of my readers would not have been born at that time, would not have experienced the fear of being invaded by a ruthless enemy, and may not realise the importance of present-day spying in the protection of Australia. We do not want Australia to ever be a battlefield.

In these pages, there are stories of murder and suicide (attempted or successful) by cyanide, arsenic, thallium, shotgun, or rifle in different towns, cities, and countries; tales of accidental problems caused by consumption of liquorice or the near collision of large ships at sea; serious stories of doctors and patients; and some lighter stories as well, along with some personal opinions. All have been chosen to entertain and teach. Some may make you laugh, some may make you sad, and some may make a big difference to your health or that of your child.

I have written this book for a number of reasons—firstly, to recount, as one of the three persons on the bridge of HMAS *Ararat*, the reason that ship nearly caused a collision of warships at sea and how it was avoided; secondly, to let the public know that, at the height of World War II, the value of spying was demonstrated when General MacArthur's Central Bureau informed all personnel who were spying upon Japanese wireless messages to and from their army, navy, and air force (including me) that the Japanese were about to change their form of Morse, and we were even informed of what the new form would be; and thirdly and most importantly, to express my disquiet at some present-day doctors' reliance upon technology for diagnosis rather than a physical examination of the patient—an examination that might often lead to an immediate and accurate diagnosis. I have surrounded these three major topics with a number of unusual true stories that will, I hope, make you read and enjoy every word. Finally, I wish to record the responsibilities of an Australian citizen and then doctor during the last half of the twentieth century.

In the process of reading these stories, most readers will learn a lot about human anatomy and its function. All but one of the stories is true; the figment of my imagination is an existing but previously unnamed condition that you will instantly recognise. The names of a small number of people are fictitious, even though their deeds may have been meritorious, and occasionally I have changed some features in order to misdirect the identification of an individual.

It is with gratitude that I thank Mike Turner for his thorough explanations of German mining off Australia's coast and how our ships undertook minesweeping. Ron Tuft and Max Quayle taught me some of the rules of the sea governing avoidance of collisions. My nephew Stuart Hibberd advised me about radio signals, and Brian Sams refreshed my memory about the art of fisticuffs. My son Christopher guided my computer involvement, and my grandson Vaughan, with consummate ease plus a great deal of time, arranged the publication of this memoir and designed its cover, while my sister-in-law Margaret Moffitt spent countless hours correcting my mistakes and advising against publishing some of my gems.

Medicine Must Wait

At the age of seventeen, having completed the NSW Leaving Certificate, I applied in November 1941 for enrolment in the faculty of medicine at the University of Sydney. Japan had not yet entered the war, and I felt no compulsion to fight in Europe, so I was untroubled by the thought of being at university whilst others fought in Europe. Anyhow, I was only seventeen years old, and conscription was still a long way off (eligibility commenced on one's eighteenth birthday, but in reality the call-up didn't happen till many months later).

My thoughts about war service underwent a U-turn, however, when within three months Japanese forces sank the American Pacific Fleet at Pearl Harbor, Darwin was bombed (more bombs were dropped on Darwin than on Pearl Harbor), Britain's newest battleships HMS *Prince of Wales* and HMS *Renown* were sunk off the coast of Malaysia, and Japanese armed forces came within a mere three hundred miles of Australia. Although still a seventeen-year-old, I knew that it was not the time to be at university. Many men, however, thought that university was the perfect place to keep away from the fighting, and a quota was therefore brought in to keep such people from flooding universities.

On 12 March 1942, W. A. Selle, registrar of the University of Sydney, wrote stating that I had been accepted into the faculty of medicine for 1942. The letter ended with the words: "If you do not intend to enter the University this year, please advise me by return post so that another candidate can be given a place."

My father understood when I told him that I wanted to fight. He said, "Son, you might get an arm shot off, and you cannot be a doctor with one arm, so I will get you a job in the bank, and you can always return as a one-armed bank clerk if that happens."

So I declined W. A. Selle's offer, and it was another twelve years before I became a doctor. The person who took my place at the University of Sydney would have been seven years senior to me when I finally became a doctor. You will understand why I dislike, with some exceptions, people who commenced university studies in 1942 or 1943 —the Japanese were in Timor and New Guinea, and Australia was fighting for its life. The danger of invasion had passed by 1944.

Within days, I was a bank clerk at the Rural Bank in Martin Place, Sydney, and broached the subject of enlistment when I turned eighteen. I was informed that the bank would not re-employ me after the war if I volunteered to join up within a year of commencing employment. So I could not enlist. However, the bank could not stop the militia from calling me up in about nine months' time, so the solution was obvious. I went to the Citizen Military Forces (CMF) recruiting centre in Manly and told the sergeant of my problem, with the result that he gave me an appointment for a medical examination on the day after my eighteenth birthday—many months earlier than it would have been.

During my last six weeks as a seventeen-year-old, I lived in Manly and commuted by ferry each day. The ride on a Manly ferry is always a joy, but the short walk from Martin Place to Circular Quay improved the return trip from the Rural Bank. The reason was a sign that cheered me up immensely. It was on the window of an office on the first floor of a building, announcing in gold letters:

SAMUEL GROCOCK ARTIFICIAL LIMB SPECIALIST

Samuel had apparently chosen his occupation as a birthright.

* * *

Having passed the army medical examination, I became a member of the CMF and altered my age in my pay book (I still have it) to nineteen years, which permitted me to transfer to the Australian Imperial Force (AIF).

My life as a spy began with my involvement in the interception of Japanese radio messages on 30 May 1942, two days after I became an Australian soldier. My eighteenth birthday had been a fortnight earlier. Some hundreds of us new recruits were sitting in a grandstand at Sydney

Showground, pencil, paper, and writing board in hand, as we faced an army version of an intelligence test—or perhaps it could be more accurately described as a lack-of-intelligence test.

No one present realised that a few kilometres away, three Japanese miniature submarines were manoeuvring to enter our harbour. Nor did we know that, at the same time in Britain, the crews of one thousand bombers were preparing for a raid of previously unsurpassed magnitude that would destroy Cologne but leave the Cologne Cathedral standing majestically amid the rubble. Four hundred and thirty-eight Germans would die within the next thirty-six hours, and London's *Daily Express* would display the headline "Vengeance Begins." Twenty-one sailors, only a mile or so from where we sat, would die from a Japanese torpedo fired in Sydney Harbour. Also, as we sat oblivious in the pavilion, an American fleet was secretly approaching Midway Island in order to ambush a Japanese invasion fleet designed to destroy American aircraft carriers.

Having been told to write our name and army number upon each sheet of paper and directed how we were to subsequently pass them for collection, we had instructions shouted at us by one of three NCOs standing by a folding table at the foreground of the stand: "The first test is a sum. Add five and four then take away three. Write your answer on the paper and pass the page to the aisle for collection."

We watched as the NCOs collected the pages and sorted them into two piles. The sergeant then took the smaller pile and called the men, one by one, to the front of the grandstand. Another NCO appeared, and the men were marched away with their destiny unstated. I felt sure that they were not destined for the Pay Corps. Australian newspapers today, seventy years later, report that our schools are neglecting mathematics as our students' ranking in the world slips ever backward, but that simple sum confirmed that it was not high in 1942.

Further tests were carried out during the day. One that I recall involved a wooden box measuring about 20 x 12 x 2.5 centimetres. There were slots in the left and right walls with a lever protruding from each slot so that the box appeared to have a left and a right arm. When the right-hand lever was pressed from the top of the box to the bottom or in the reverse direction, the left one moved in exactly the same direction. Our task was to draw a diagram of the mechanism concealed within the box.

At the end of the day, about thirty of us were told that we were to join a new signals unit that had been formed less than two weeks previously, and within days we were in Bonegilla camp as members of Australian Special Wireless Group (ASWG), a unit with a nucleus of about thirty men who had just returned to Australia after fighting the Germans, Italians, and Vichy French in the Middle East. Their task had been to intercept enemy wireless messages, and after escaping from Greece and Crete, they were involved in the campaign in Syria before being converted to Japanese Morse code (kana). They had come back to Australia to create a new unit.

We were joined by equal numbers of teenagers arriving from Victoria and Queensland to complete the wireless operator component of the unit. We were soon informed that ours was a secret unit and that, as we now knew of its existence and duties, we could not be transferred to any other unit or service. Furthermore, we were forbidden to disclose the existence of the unit for fifty years. Later, many members of the Australian Women's Army Service (AWAS) were to join the unit, and they intercepted Japanese messages from ASWG stations in Perth, Brisbane, and Melbourne.

We were taught International Morse Code, and then a handful of very nice Pommies taught us Japanese kana. Some of these Pommies had been monitoring the Japanese since 1935 in Hong Kong and escaped just before the Japanese invaded. My training in Japanese wireless interception at Kalinga, a suburb of Brisbane, continued into early 1943. For a short period, I was sent to our direction finding (DF) team at Bald Hill. The work there was boring but important, in that we were establishing bearings on Japanese radio stations in the Pacific area whilst another DF station was undertaking the same procedure from Western Australia. Where the bearings crossed was the site of the Japanese transmitter. I was told by other members of the team that Central Bureau would sometimes urgently request a bearing upon an illegal transmitter in Australia sending messages to the Japanese.

Within a year I was transferred, with eleven other operators, to Darwin via Townsville. Australia's womenfolk were helping the troops in hundreds of different ways—from making camouflage netting to knitting socks— but I will never forget the dedication of the women of Bowen, just south of Townsville. Thousands of troops were passing through for embarkation in Townsville to New Guinea and elsewhere, and all were greeted by these ladies with cheery smiles, food, and drinks. Many trestle tables adorned Bowen railway station as each troop train arrived. We were soon to learn of a different kind of Australian civilian when we reached Townsville: wharfies.

Our train disgorged us at Oonoomba, a suburb of Townsville, soon after dark in early 1943, and some hundreds of us carried our worldly possessions as we slowly ascended a gravel ridge above an army camp in a gully to our left. Campfires glowed and no one spoke as a beautiful tenor voice rose in song from the darkness below.

We were confined to Oonoomba transit camp for some days and not permitted into Townsville city because, we were informed, army troops had seriously assaulted some Townsville wharf labourers, and bayonets were involved. It was 2014 before I was to read a sickening account of this clash with the Townsville wharf labourers when I read Hal Colebach's *Australia's Secret War*, detailing how Australian wharf labourers at most Australian ports were sabotaging and rendering useless equipment for Allied troops fighting the Japanese. They deliberately smashed aeroplanes, equipment was rendered useless by damage or theft of vital components— everything possible was done to assist the Japanese who were endeavouring to invade Australia.

Furthermore, the wharfies demanded treble or even quadruple pay as "danger money" when handling war materials and were frequently on strike and refusing to load ships, including those of our navy. All Australians should read *Australia's Secret War*. Some people question its accuracy, but I can vouch for the fact that Australian army soldiers had to fight Townsville wharfies at a time when Japanese troops were three hundred miles away.

The train ride to Mount Isa was interrupted when an American serviceman, as we trundled between Charters Towers and Mount Isa, lost his balance while surfing a carriage roof and was killed. Leaving the train, we travelled in the back of trucks for hundreds of miles and then in cattle trucks on another railway in the Northern Territory to finally arrive as a re-enforcement to 51 Wireless Section, situated about seventy kilometres south of Darwin. The wireless interception unit was at Coomalie Creek adjacent to the 31 Squadron airfield, home to the Bristol Beaufighters. (The Japanese called the Beaufighters "whispering death" owing to their habit of suddenly appearing over Japanese airfields in Timor with their four cannons and six machine guns blazing.)

The wireless operators at 51 Wireless Section knew that there would be an air raid upon Darwin the night I arrived, but they did not realise that it would include an attack on the airfield adjacent to us and would therefore be a danger to us. Their anticipation of the raid was due to traffic analysis in which the quantity, origin, and destination of Japanese messages indicated the intention of the Japanese without the content of their messages being known. On this occasion and subsequently, the knowledge of an impending bombing attack upon Darwin was made because Japanese bombers stationed in Kendari (Sulawesi), out of reach of our bombers, had flown to Koepang (Timor) the previous evening, their wireless/air gunners filling the airwaves with messages that 51 Wireless Section operators had intercepted. It did not require a genius to determine that the Japanese movement of bombers to within easy reach of Darwin indicated their intention to attack the following night. Experience had led the men to recognise that a full moon added to the certainty of an attack.

The expectation of an air raid did not deter the old soldiers whom I had joined, and I was escorted to the weekly picture show in the early evening. After a walk of about a kilometre on a dirt track, we arrived at the theatre—a clearing with the removed tree trunks aligned to form rows of seating. A huge canvas strung tightly between poles was the screen. The movie having finished, we commenced the return to our camp accompanied by a siren, which the old soldiers informed me was a yellow warning that Japanese bombers were in the vicinity. Nobody was alarmed.

Half an hour later, the red alarm sounded. I was standing in our camp, the moonlight displaying against the night sky the beauty of the slim trunk and bushy head of the silver oaks. It was very peaceful except for the Japanese bombers—which, I remarked to Jack Esson, sounded like trucks on a mountain road. Someone said that the reason for the sound was that the engines were not synchronised, but that was meaningless to me.

The planes were not directly above us, and I stood in the open with Jack and another soldier whilst the other members of 51 Section moved sensibly into the slit trenches. I was not being a hero; it was clear to me that there was no immediate danger if the old soldiers were not in the trenches, which were nearby. Suddenly, the other two heard the sound made by

Japanese bombers when releasing bombs, and they were in full flight to the slit trenches. But so was I—in the opposite direction to trenches also close by. A split second later, as I reached a trench, a Japanese flare burst above us, lighting up everything like daylight, and I saw the crouched, bare back of Fred Pakes blocking where I had intended to jump. So I ran a few paces to the next trench and jumped into it as bombs exploded between the airstrip and us.

My friend Jack Banks, later to hold a senior position in the Commonwealth Bank in Melbourne, received Jack Esson and a retaining pole upon his back as he stooped, also bare-chested, in a trench. He subsequently claimed to have been shaking for the following three weeks because he had thought the simultaneous sound of exploding bombs and a violent assault upon his shirtless back indicated a bomb had joined him in his trench.

My fellow soldiers had built our set room upon a small knoll. Trees had been felled from our campsite and used to construct the framework. The roof was corrugated iron, and the metre high-walls were made of local pandanus palms. Twelve operators, each with two of the latest American wireless sets, occupied the two long sides, and as one group completed their shift, another would commence. High aerials were close by.

Our headphones were not placed over our ears but forward of them, because this gave the clearest sound. Our left hands rested lightly upon the dial of the set directly in front of us while our right hands recorded the message being sent by the Japanese operator. We had been trained to be writing the letter or numeral two removed from the one that was being transmitted, which meant that we were always concentrating upon three symbols; we were simultaneously writing the first letter heard, remembering the second, and listening to the third until the message had been completed.

We were all very good operators. I can remember that on a number of occasions, whilst recording a Japanese message, there would be a burst of static that smothered one symbol of a letter, a dit or a dah, but my brain would automatically write an interpretation, even though I knew I had not heard whether a dit or a dah had been sent. The second Japanese operator would always miss the same letter and request a repeat, which invariably confirmed that what I had written was correct, even though I knew that I had not heard the sound sent.

I now realise that my brain was not only measuring the duration of the sounds sent but also the duration of the silences between sounds; therefore, when a single sound was obliterated, my brain (and other operators' brains) knew immediately that the total duration of sounds heard could only have been consistent with either a dit or a dah being obliterated by static. My brain had determined that the time missed by static was equal to either a dit bracketed by the usual silent periods or a dah plus the silent periods.

The Japanese used dits and dahs as in International Morse Code, but with totally different meanings. Furthermore, their alphabet consists of seventy-five combinations, which are long and complicated. For example the equal longest combination in the international code is *dah dah dit dah*, meaning the letter *q*. But one that I regularly heard from a Japanese was *dah dah dit dit dah dit dit dah dah dit*. One that I was anxious to hear but never did was sent from Japanese planes: *dah dit dit dit dit dah dah dah*. In international code, that is *nij*, but to the Japanese, I was informed, it meant that the plane was landing or crashing. If it was sent near Darwin, it meant crashing into the Arafura Sea.

The Japanese were very fast Morse operators, sending their messages at between twenty-two and thirty words per minute—which was fine for our operators who were recording the messages by pencil. If kana was used, we had plenty of time to record the symbol, but if the Japanese operator was using an abbreviated form and sending at the usual speed in excess of twenty-five words per minute, we commonly were forced to use a type of shorthand. For example, *t* was represented by a dash, *m* by a half moon, and *n* by a single upright.

Within less than a year, we were informed that the Japanese were about to make a major change in the form of Morse used in one of their major traffics and exactly what form the new messages would take. I was astounded that our intelligence services could give us this kind of information.

A fortnight passed, and I was writing down the messages being sent by a Japanese operator when, after sending a message, both he and the Japanese communicating with him, suddenly disappeared. My search for the two Japanese commenced immediately. I slowly turned the dial of one wireless set listening to every station. At last, I recognised the tone of the first transmitter.

I then searched for the second Japanese with my other wireless and found both of them within fifteen minutes. Of course, as well as being on new frequencies, they were using new call signs and were transmitting a new form of Morse—but as far as I was concerned, we were back in business, and I was as competent as they at the new Morse. Some of the eleven operators with me on duty at that time had been similarly occupied; and so we had, within about half an hour, found the new frequencies of the Japanese radio transmitters that we were monitoring.

It is said that some wireless operators are recognisable to other experienced operators by their *fist*—their characteristic manner of operating a Morse key. But we identified the Japanese transmitters by their individual tones, not by the operators' fists. Every Japanese radio transmitter had its own individual sound, which was usually as recognisable as your mother's voice and was due, I am told, to a number of things, such as the capacitor, inductor electronics, the rise time and decay time of the signal, the power supply, and the aerial.

Failure to recognise the changed tone of Japanese naval signals contributed, I suspect, to the destruction of the American fleet at Pearl Harbor. Admiral Yamamoto completely deceived the Americans into believing that the aircraft carrier *Akagi* and her large fleet of accompanying vessels were in Japanese waters when in fact they were in the Pacific Ocean, about to bomb unsuspecting peacetime Pearl Harbor. That is indisputable. The *Akagi* fleet had been under strict radio silence while another ship or ships, remaining in Japanese waters, pretended to be the *Akagi* as it sent numerous fake radio messages on *Akagi's* radio frequencies.

Numerous investigations have confirmed that Yamamoto removed the *Akagi* wireless operators from the *Akagi* and used them on his fake fleet in order to preserve the fist of the operators on the fake *Akagi*, and this has been claimed to be the reason that the deception was successful. I don't believe it, because it was the tone of the Japanese transmitter, not the fist of its operator, that we wireless interceptors recognised, as I have described above.

The question is why the American wireless operators did not detect the sudden change in tone of the *Akagi* transmitter when the real *Akagi* ceased transmitting and the imposter commenced. Only the three or four American operators monitoring the *Akagi* were or are capable of giving the answer as to why they did not notice a change in tone of the Akagi's transmitter. Anyone else is guessing, and those opinions are worthless. I suspect that the Americans, not being at war, may have only undertaken intermittent monitoring of the real *Akagi*, with the result being that the wireless operators did not become familiar with the real *Akagi*'s wireless tone and therefore failed to recognize the change of tone when the fake *Akagi* commenced sending messages on the real *Akagi*'s wireless frequency.

I know that multiple investigations have been undertaken in order to determine how the Hawaii wireless interceptors failed to warn America that a new transmitter was operating on the *Akagi* frequency and that the real *Akagi* was therefore missing, but I have no knowledge of their conclusions. As far as I am concerned, the blame lies absolutely with the wireless operators or their superiors. It is absolutely indisputable that they did not detect the changed tone in the new transmitter, and there could only have been a limited number of reasons for this crucial failure.

The most likely reason, as previously stated, is that the *Akagi* was not being monitored all day and every day during the month prior to the attack on Pearl Harbor, and therefore the operators would not have been familiar with the tone of its transmitter and could not be blamed for the lack of planning. Secondly, they may have recognized the change in tone but thought nothing of it and failed to report it. Thirdly, they may have reported it but the intelligence section, not realizing its significance, failed to pass the fact on to higher authorities.

I found my two elusive Japanese transmitters by searching the airwaves for their unique tones and finding them on new frequencies, carrying a new form of Morse and under different call signs. How different might the attack on Pearl Harbor have been if the change in *Akagi*'s transmitter had been noticed? How many American lives would have been saved then and later, and how many ships would have remained afloat? It is sobering to reflect that radio-fingerprinting, invented by the British earlier in the same year, would have positively identified the transmitters as fakes and could have led to the surreptitious attack being anticipated. It might even have led to the American fleet ambushing the Japanese rather than being tied up to wharves as sitting ducks. Fanciful?

Spying is the world's second oldest profession, eclipsed only by the marginally less dangerous profession of prostitution. Some Australians see spying as an infringement of civil liberties. Many uninformed people, for example, asked how Australia could be a friend to Indonesia yet at the same time tap the private mobile phones of that country's leader and his wife. In response, then Australian Prime Minister Tony Abbott said that spying is a way of life for all countries and as such is universally undertaken in the best interests of that country's citizens. He is, of course, correct. All countries undertake spying to the best of their abilities. It is insurance against unexpected attack.

Fortunately, certain British, Australian, and American individuals recognised, from as early as 1920, that Japan was a future enemy and that every effort should be made to learn to speak and read Japanese fluently in order to decode and decipher that country's communications. No one man can be singled out as the leader, but Eric Nave is undoubtedly the best-known Australian involved in interception of Japanese wireless messages and the breaking of their codes. His revelations of Japanese capabilities and intentions saved countless Australian, British, and American lives during World War II and were only possible because he had spent twenty years studying the Japanese language, codes, and ciphers.

The Royal Australian Navy had posted him to Japan in 1920 for the express purpose of mastering the Japanese language, and by 1925 he was already involved in deciphering their codes and ciphers. His expertise became known to the British, who used his skills at Bletchley Park before he returned to Australia to continue his interception work on Japanese codes and ciphers before and during the war. The British were involved in intercepting Japanese wireless messages and cryptanalysis from the early 1920s, but to a lesser extent after the war with Germany turned their attention more to that country's messages. The American navy also was deeply involved in this form of spying upon Japan from at least the early 1930s, with the American army only becoming deeply involved after the advent of war in the Pacific.

Secrecy about our spying is obviously of national importance, yet today we see Assange and Snowden carrying on as though they are the saviours of the free world. Have they saved a single life? How many people have been killed because of their disclosures? Is there any remote possibility that the harm they have done is outweighed by something good that has come from their disclosures? Our next generation may pay dearly for the actions of those two self-righteous individuals who have exposed our country's secrets to the world and created unwarranted enmity in our neighbours.

One of our guardian angels is the Australian Signals Directorate, which was exposed by Snowden for monitoring the mobile phone of the wife of the president of Indonesia and for recording the telephone activity (traffic analysis only—not listening to conversations) of Islamic jihadists planning to kill as many Australians as possible before they themselves were killed at Holsworthy Barracks. Had the Australian Signals Directorate not been active, a number of innocent Australians would very definitely have been murdered at Holsworthy.

Spying by our country is essential for your protection.

The Sea Is a Dangerous Place

Germany recognised the strategic importance of shipping in Australian waters, and on 15 June 1940—eighteen months prior to Japan's entry into World War II—the German raider/minelayer *Pinguin* left Germany bound for the Indian Ocean and Australia with her holds filled with mines. She captured a Norwegian tanker *Storstad* on 7 October in the Indian Ocean, converted her to a minelayer by transferring 110 mines in mid-ocean, and renamed her *Passat*. The two ships then set course for the east coast of Australia.

They separated and *Pinguin* dropped forty mines on anchors between Sydney and Newcastle on 28–29 October 1940, while *Passat* anchored thirty in Banks Strait and forty at the eastern entrance to Bass Strait. While *Passat* was dropping another forty at the western end of Bass Strait, *Pinguin* was laying forty off Hobart. More were laid in the Spencer Gulf.

These German mines soon had victims, with Britain's SS *Cambridge* being sunk on 7 November 1940 about six miles off Wilson's Promontory. The next day, the first ship bearing American registration was sunk in World War II: *City of Rayville*, about six miles from Cape Otway. One of the mines anchored by *Pinguin* near Newcastle later broke its chains and lay fully exposed but unrecognised for more than fifty years amongst the rocks at a favourite fishing spot, Broughton Island. Recognised at last, it was detonated.

The German ships reunited in the Indian Ocean, and *Passat* successfully reached Bordeaux on 4 February 1941. But *Pinguin* was sunk by HMS *Cornwall*. When Germany surrendered in May 1945, the documents from *Passat* were given to the Royal Australian Navy, and clearance of the German mines commenced. After Japan was defeated, minesweeping continued. By sheer chance, and although I was a soldier not a sailor, I was a participant upon HMAS *Ararat* in January 1946 at the ripe old age of twenty-one.

Sub-Lieutenant Thomas Eckett Edwards, RAN, a school friend, was assigned to HMAS *Ararat* as one of five officers, and in June–July 1943, the ship was tied up to a pier in Brisbane where I, as an eighteen-year-old signalman in Australian Special Wireless Group (ASWG), spent some pleasant evenings in the ship's wardroom drinking small quantities of duty-free alcohol and chatting to Tom and his officer friends. All of us, except for the commander—a lieutenant—had been schoolboys eighteen months previously.

Later, I was to again spend time in their mess when HMAS *Ararat* visited Darwin, where I was intercepting Japanese army, navy and air force wireless messages. Neither the young men on HMAS *Ararat* nor I, on that day in 1944, could have imagined that, twenty years later, HMAS *Ararat*, being decommissioned, would return to Darwin Harbour under Japanese ownership to undertake salvage of ships sunk by the Japanese during the war.

The Japanese surrender in August 1945 did not mean that all servicemen could go home. There was a strict demobilisation framework that allotted points to each serviceman. The more points held, the sooner the serviceman was discharged. Duration of service was obviously of prime importance in the allocation of points, but other factors—such as age and marital state—influenced one's total. An old bloke of thirty-five years who was married was quickly back home and in the workforce, while his unmarried twenty-five-year-old mate would wear a uniform for many more months.

Although I had joined the army within a fortnight of reaching eighteen and had served for three and a half years at war's end, I was still only twenty-one and unmarried, so my points were low. I was destined to stay in the army for more than another year. My friend Tom, under the same rules, was retained in the navy on HMAS *Ararat*, with his duties including the clearing of minefields.

I was transferred to Mornington in Victoria and spent each day listening to and writing down wireless messages sent by Russians in International Morse Code. So much for being our allies a few months earlier; now we were spying on them. My life as a wireless spy merely changed from intercepting Japanese wireless messages to intercepting Russian ones.

HMAS *Ararat*, with Tom as the Asdic officer (*sonar* is the word more commonly used today), arrived in Melbourne soon after my transfer to Victoria and was tied up at Station Pier in Port Philip. Tom was scheduled to commence minesweeping in Bass Strait as a member of the 20th Mine Sweeping Flotilla during the last fortnight of January 1946.

During early January, Tom and I met in Mornington, and he told me that he might be able to arrange for me to accompany him minesweeping as a guest in the officers' mess of HMAS *Ararat,* if I could get leave from my unit. Unbelievable: here I was, an AIF signalman, being offered a trip to sea in the officers' quarters of a warship.

I soon had a pass for five days' leave from ASWG and was firmly ensconced on the *Ararat* as the 20th flotilla (HMAS *Swan,* HMAS *Warrnambool,* HMAS *Ararat,* HMAS *Bunbury,* HMAS *Katoomba,* HMAS *Lithgow* and HMAS *Townsville*) sailed from Port Philip. I was seated at the dining table with the officers as we sailed, in late afternoon, out from Port Philip into the ocean with the renowned swell playing havoc with my equilibrium. I remember the ship and my body pitching forwards then backwards, backwards then forwards, while simultaneously, on the bulkhead in front of me, a large painting of the king rolled left to right, right to left. It was too much for my innate gyroscope to manage, and I rushed from the wardroom amid laughter from my hosts.

Of course, I knew that my trip to sea could take as long as a fortnight and that there would be trouble awaiting me when I finally reported back to my army unit, but I was not bothered by that small technicality. My five days' leave was soon expended, but as I could not swim back to my army base, I had to put up with life on board the corvette. What a holiday! Better than any cruise ship. To be AWL (absent without leave) during war years was a serious matter, but the war was over, and recording Russian messages was not a priority. I suffered no guilt.

It was known from *Passat*'s charts where she had placed mines in batches of five or ten, with the mines about a kilometre apart, but the batches were separated by many kilometres, thus giving a wide coverage of the ocean. The Royal Australian Navy's plan was, as far as I can determine, to sweep these areas in tracts that were about ten kilometres wide and fifteen or so kilometres long, therefore allowing a big margin for German error in recording the exact area of the minefield.

One ship was to act as the *danbuoy layer*—i.e., it would drop a row of buoys parallel to but outside the left-hand side of the minefield. HMAS *Ararat* was the danbuoy layer and therefore the leading ship in the actual minesweeping. She was followed by HMAS *Swan*, slightly bigger as a sloop, which would make the initial sweep, keeping *Ararat's* marker buoys close to her port side but, as with *Ararat*, being outside the estimated minefield.

HMAS *Swan*, like all the other corvettes, had an Oropesa sweep extending starboard underwater from her stern to a submerged paravane two hundred metres away on the right-hand side. The Oropesa sweep was a serrated cable designed to cut the chains of any mines in its path so that they could rise to the surface and be destroyed by rifle fire. The other five corvettes, with their Oropesa sweeps similarly extending two hundred metres to their right, would follow each other just inside the safety of the preceding ship's paravane. Thus, each pass of the six ships was sweeping a strip of ocean many kilometres long and at least a kilometre wide.

HMAS *Ararat*, having retrieved the original line of danbouys whilst the other six ships were undertaking the actual minesweeping, would then lay the next line of marker buoys just inside and behind the safety of the sixth ship's Oropesa sweep. The clearance of the adjacent strip of ocean would then be undertaken. Obviously, a very good lookout was maintained to detect any mine cut loose by the preceding ship's sweep suddenly rising to the surface in front of the next-in-line ship.

All days aboard that vessel were memorable, but one day more than others for a very particular reason. There were four of us on the bridge *of* HMAS *Ararat* when the day's minesweeping came to an end: the captain, whose rank was lieutenant; a sub-lieutenant, whom we will call Peter; the sailor steering the *Ararat*; and me. Our bow was pointing in the direction of HMAS *Swan*, which was probably ten or so kilometres away and leading her cygnets towards us in a line-astern formation.

The skipper said to the other officer, "Steer [a compass bearing] and fall in behind the *Swan*."

Those were his words, and it was clear to me that we would allow the line of six ships to pass us and then do a U-turn to take up the position of last ship in a row of seven. Clear as crystal and no room for error, you may think—but think again. Peter had a different interpretation of what the skipper had said. The skipper left the bridge, and we sailed on a smooth sea on a lovely summer's afternoon. What a joy it was to be alive—the joy enhanced by the knowledge that I should be sitting in front of high-powered radios recording Russian messages that probably no one would read.

The other ships drew closer. It was apparent to all that they would pass on our port side; and then, as we drew level with the *Swan*, Peter gave the order for the *Ararat* to make a 90-degree turn and charge directly at the line of other ships. I could not believe it; he had misinterpreted the order. He thought that his instruction had been to insert HMAS *Ararat* between the leading ship, HMAS *Swan*, and the second ship, and so become the second ship in the line rather than to let them all pass us and then fall in behind them as the last ship.

All ships would have been travelling at about twelve knots, so HMAS *Ararat*, of 650 tons displacement, at a speed of twenty-two kilometres an hour, with no brakes, was commencing a U-turn in the middle of the ocean in order to insert itself between two other ships doing the same speed in the opposite direction. Madness. Death was staring me in the face.

"Holy fuck, Peter, the skipper meant at the end of the line, not here," was my anxious cry.

He did not answer me but immediately issued further orders, which resulted in us commencing and then completing a tight full circle to return to our original course parallel to, but in the opposite direction of, the other ships.

We were in the anticlockwise full circle when the skipper burst onto the bridge, his face covered in shaving cream. I cannot recall the conversation, but I do remember my sense of relief on seeing the line of ships again on our port side rather than directly ahead of our bow. Not a cloud in the sky, the sun shining brightly, the ocean as smooth as a lake, visibility clear—but human error never far away!

Many would have been on the bridges of the six other ships, and many would have been saying "Holy fuck" as they watched *Ararat* suddenly do a left-hand turn and charge directly at their line. Wide-eyed, they would have been planning what action they would take within the next minute or two to keep their own ship from being involved in a multi-ship collision. I suppose they had been trained in handling just such an event. Not a single ship wavered: all held the line. Great discipline.

Of course, all officers would have known the *International Regulations for Preventing Collisions at Sea*, and all would have been aware that HMAS *Ararat*, having the other ship on her starboard side, was obliged not to attempt crossing ahead of her. Therefore, they would have been expecting and praying that HMAS *Ararat* would complete a tight anticlockwise circle and resume her original course. Thankfully, that is what we did.

Not wishing to put its message onto the airwaves for the world to read and question, HMAS *Swan* sent a visual message, which Tom informed me later read, "Nice manoeuvre, *Ararat*." Sarcasm, no doubt, but who cared? We were afloat. We finally did a U-turn at the appropriate time and place and became the last ship in the line as we proceeded to Wilson's Promontory, where we anchored for the night.

There were nearly six hundred crew on those seven ships that day, and the conversation in the messes that night would have been highly interesting, with only three men—the helmsman of HMAS *Ararat*, the officer, and me—knowing all the facts. Some would be telling the story today without knowing why HMAS *Ararat* did a pirouette in front of the flotilla.

This near collision of warships occurred because an officer attempted to undertake the exact order given: "Fall in behind the *Swan*," although common sense should have told him that those words meant "Fall in behind the Swan *group*."

When I returned to camp, I was of course immediately arrested for having been AWL. I was solemnly marched, hatless, between guards with unloaded rifles, before the adjutant, who said, "Signalman Moffitt, due to an oversight, you were granted five days' leave when you were only entitled to two days, but you then took another nine days AWL. Have you anything to say?"

"Sir, I have been a guest in the officers' mess of HMAS *Ararat* of the 20th Minesweeping Flotilla sweeping Bass Strait for mines laid by the Germans at the beginning of the war. But I thought it would only be a day trip and was surprised to be gone for nearly a fortnight."

The war was over, and the adjutant couldn't think of a suitable punishment, so I received a reprimand only.

"Dismissed," he said as he gazed at some documents on his desk. The two guards and I turned left and marched out in single file.

The adjutant was probably thinking, *Lucky bastard. I hope he invites me on his next trip.*

A Doctor at Last

My army life changed in 1946 when I was based at Mornington Racecourse intercepting Russian high-speed diplomatic messages, recording them on Edison wax cylinders, and then slowing them down for transcription. I don't know where they went, but the work was low-key and unsupervised.

I had married a trained nurse of Scottish extraction whom I met in Brisbane when based there at war's end. I was now renting a house and owned, for a short time, a beautiful 1928 Silver Anniversary Buick Coupe. These extra expenses required more cash, which I obtained by working as a house painter between wireless shifts. The owner paid my army mate and me ninety-five pounds to paint the Mornington Swimming Baths. They were destroyed by fire shortly afterwards.

Penniless, married, a civilian again, I became a medical student by courtesy of the Department of Veteran Affairs. It was to be "survival of the fittest," as about a thousand medical students enrolled at the faculty of medicine, University of Sydney, in 1947.

One hundred and fifty found the course to be beyond them and quickly dropped out, leaving about eight hundred and fifty of us to do the first-year medical examinations. The subsequent yearly failure rate was always significant, but concomitantly, people who had failed the higher year's examinations replaced some of the losses. Six years after we started, only 272 graduated, but many of these had commenced at least one year earlier than the rest of us. About 25 per cent of we originals passed the six-year course unscathed.

The outstanding student over the six years, the man who was awarded the University Medal, was Alan Hoyle, who was older than most of us. He had been a POW of the Japanese and had not completed high school when he joined the army. He could have chosen any path in medicine, but he chose general practice, and of course set a high standard in a suburb of Newcastle. From prisoner of war to University Medallist in Medicine: what an accomplishment.

My six years were good but hard. The eldest of my three sons was born, and our allowance was supplemented in numerous ways. Sometimes my wife undertook casual nursing. I painted houses around Manly. We took in boarders. To save money, I used public transport or hitchhiked to university. I would pay the car driver's Harbour Bridge toll, which was six pence for car and driver plus three pence for each passenger, so I paid nine pence. I recall a paediatrician from the Royal Alexandra Hospital for Children picking me up in an expensive car one day. When he heard that I was a medical student, he gave me a lecture on the ethics of medicine and hitchhiking. I suspected that he had avoided war service by being at university during the war, but he was not all bad. He had given me a lift, and such people were uncommon.

Life is full of mysteries. After six intense years of study, I was sitting beside another mature-age student in a lecture room containing about two hundred students when he said to me, "You know, Paul, I believe that all disease is caused by constipation." It is a mystery to me how someone could make such a statement after six years of studying medicine. What hope would his patients have? Within months, we were doctors, but in different hospitals. Theory became practice, and his superiors would have quickly dispelled that belief.

Just Another Day in General Practice

Except for a few months in 1946, I had never had enough money to possess a car—even though, at twenty-nine, I was a doctor at the Royal Prince Alfred Hospital. A junior doctor today earns a fortune, but we, in 1953, were paid a pittance. It was time for me to seek a better source of income. I entered general practice in partnership with two others in an already established practice in Cessnock. My patients were coal miners, and 99 per cent of them were wonderful, uncomplicated people. These were happy days.

All roads out of Cessnock were gravel, and the nearest large hospital—along with physicians, surgeons, and obstetricians—was in Newcastle, which was reached by eighteen miles of gravel to Maitland and then about twenty miles of bitumen to Newcastle. We general practitioners, therefore, had to be jacks-of-all-trades, and each day was a learning experience. A wrong diagnoses could have dire consequences, and every one of the dozen GPs in town was competent and serious.

To add to our commitment, we were available day and night and did many home visits each day as well as hospital visits, emergency medicine, and planned surgery. I delivered ninety-two babies in 1960 and the same number in 1961. In truth, the obstetrics-trained nurse delivered the babies (the actual delivery is normally not as important as the months of supervision before delivery), with the doctor giving a light anaesthetic and only taking charge if a forceps delivery was required. Specialists from Newcastle would come to our hospital to operate or advise in an emergency that was beyond our expertise and also for difficult planned surgery on Monday, our allotted operating day.

Mr Slipped Disc

It had been a normal day, so I would have seen approximately forty patients in my consulting room, another five to ten in hospital, and a further seven in their homes. It was about eight thirty at night, and one of my partners and I had just been joined at the local hospital by a neurosurgeon from Newcastle. I had called him to operate on the skull of the grandfather of a male who would become one of Australia's best-known murderers; the grandson and his accomplice used a captive woman's forehead for target practice and one chided the other when his bullet was one centimetre off centre. They had raped her, of course. (His application for release was again refused in 2015.)

I had met the grandfather, for the first time, the previous day, after a thirty-kilometre drive to his property. His daughter had said to me, "I don't know what is wrong with Dad. He fell off a horse six weeks ago and has been off-colour ever since. Some days he is his old self, but other days he is lethargic and says that his arm is weak."

It took no brains to diagnose what that meant. The patient had a subdural haematoma and required a burr hole into his skull to remove the blood clot and the fluid it had absorbed. I admitted him to hospital and made the arrangement for the Newcastle- based neurosurgeon to operate the following evening.

Later the same day, I saw a miner with a slipped disc. As with the farmer, his diagnosis was absolutely simple. He had fallen as he walked into the coal mine on the previous day and had immediately experienced a lower back pain that had subsequently extended down one leg and into his foot. It was worsened by bending, coughing, and defecating. I had admitted him in order to give pain relief and to confirm the obvious diagnosis with an X-ray of his lumbar vertebrae. He had not been a good patient and had given the nursing staff some grief with his persistence in remaining absolutely immobile, even to the extent of requiring catheterisation to empty his bladder.

The neurosurgeon commenced the operation on the head of the man with a haematoma with a curving incision behind, above, and in front of one ear in order to expose the skull, as the skin and subcutaneous tissues were freed from the bone. A trephine then drilled a two-centimetre hole into the bone to expose the brain—surrounded, as expected, by abnormal fluid. During the surgery, we gossiped, and I mentioned the patient with the slipped disc.

"I would love to see him. I have a special interest in slipped discs," said the surgeon, as the bloodstained haematoma was sucked from around the brain. The operation all but complete, I sewed up the wound, and my partner joined us as we visited the man with the slipped disc.

Television was yet to arrive in Australia, and so twenty sets of bored eyes turned towards us as we entered the ward—those of the trained nurse and nineteen patients. The twentieth patient, the one with the slipped disc, was lying on his back and unaware of our approach. Introductions over, the surgeon, who had been told the history, asked a few questions before sitting close by the patient's head and intoning, "Shortly you will become tired, and you will shut your eyes and drift off to sleep."

What the fuck is happening? I wondered. It was my introduction to hypnotism.

"I will count," said the surgeon, "and you will awaken on ten."

And so there were twenty-three sets of eyes watching as the previously immobile patient, having been instructed to do so, rolled over. The large surgeon, having carefully positioned his hands upon the patient's lower back, exerted sudden downward pressure. Responding to instructions, the patient arose from his bed, voided into a urinal, walked the length of the ward, returned to, and reclined upon his bed. I was speechless.

The counting began, and the patient opened his eyes at ten. Upon questioning, he stated that his severe pain had gone.

We returned to the Doctors' Room for a midnight coffee. The surgeon, responding to our expressions of amazement at the recent hypnosis, remarked, "All you have to do is get somebody less intelligent than yourself. Here, Jim," he said to my partner, "let me have a go at you."

My partner was more likely to have broken the tactless and mistaken surgeon's jaw than lapse into hypnosis, and the evening ended. I finally undressed in the dark and climbed into bed unaware that my dealings with Mr Slipped Disc were far from over.

Some weeks later, Mr SD, whom I had referred to an orthopaedic surgeon, stated that the visiting Coal Mines Insurance doctor had refused him compensation. There could not be a clearer case of traumatic lumbar disc injury, and I could not understand the reason behind that doctor's decision, but I was soon to find out.

The case was held in Newcastle Court House, and I wasted a day to give my version of what seemed to be an open-and-shut case: a fall in a coal mine and its consequences. My evidence given, I chose to wait and listen to the evidence of the Coal Mines Insurance doctor.

Trained to be suspicious, he was more interested in the cause of the injury than I had been and had learned of X-rays (the existence of which were unknown to me) taken two days before the patient had supposedly fallen at the coal mine. These earlier X-rays were an IVP (intravenous pyelogram), an X-ray of the patient's kidneys, taken at the request of his usual GP, who had suspected kidney stones as the cause of the man's back pain—which had been present for much longer than he had told me. The radiologist reported normal kidneys but the presence of a slipped disc.

It was clear that the true story was quite different from the one that I had been told by the patient. The man, having been informed by the GP that his pain was due to a slipped disc and not a kidney stone, was confronted with many weeks off work on unpaid sick leave, plus the medical expenses. His future was financially grim indeed. The solution was easy: he had to fake an accident at the coal mine the next day, get a new and stupid GP, tell him a bullshit story about a fall at work, and claim compensation from the coal mine. He faked the accident and found the stupid GP (me), but the Coal Mines Insurance doctor brought him undone.

Naturally, the insurance company won the case.

I had been stupid for not asking myself why the miner, whom I had never previously met, had chosen me to treat a serious injury rather than whatever doctor had been treating him prior to the injury. I never saw him after the day in court, so I suppose he blamed me for not winning the court case. No doubt he returned to the care of the doctor who could not tell the difference between a kidney stone and a slipped lumbar disc. They deserved one another.

The Things We Do

Each month, I would medically assess Mabel Lesser and endeavour to feel the infant curled up in her immense abdomen. I did not anticipate problems with the pregnancy—she'd had, as I recall, nine or ten living infants—and I certainly did not expect the phone call I received one evening when she was nearing term.

"Mabel is bleeding from her front passage," said the caller.

I was awaiting her in the obstetrics department of the hospital when the ambulance arrived fifteen minutes later. I confirmed that a small amount of blood was running from her vagina, but she was well, and the baby's heart sounds were fine. Clearly, she had placenta praevia, which meant that, by pure bad luck, the placenta or afterbirth had been growing for the previous nine months close to the exit of the uterus and was now overlapping it. If events were allowed to proceed, the placenta would precede the infant out of the uterus, and infant death would occur.

A caesarean section on this obese female was way beyond my capabilities, so I telephoned an obstetrician in Newcastle and asked for help. He was "nature's gentleman" if ever there was one; he lived to help other people, and he immediately left his home to undertake the one-hour drive to our hospital, knowing that there would be no payment to him.

My partner and I greeted him at the door of the hospital when he arrived at about eleven that night. He confirmed the diagnosis, and we adjourned to the operating theatre change room while Mabel was transferred to the theatre. He and I spoke as we stood in front of hand basins, meticulously scrubbing our hands and lower forearms under running water, theatre caps on our heads, masks covering our faces, our shoes covered by slippers. Sterile gowns and rubber gloves would be donned after scrubbing was complete. My partner was in the adjacent operating theatre commencing Mabel's anaesthetic. Everyone was tense—except the obstetrician.

"How is the practice going, son?" he asked me, a thirty-five-year-old veteran of World War II.

"Great," I replied. "I have repaid my bank loan."

"Oh God, son," he said. "You should always owe money—that's the way you make money."

Unfortunately, it was time to move into the operating theatre, so I never did receive the pearls of wisdom that could have influenced my financial future.

The obstetrician was an artist, and he soon pulled a living infant from Mabel's uterus, then gave me an anatomy lesson as he meticulously sewed the uterus and all of the layers of Mabel's gigantic abdomen together. I particularly remember him saying, "Those are the pyramidalis muscles, Paul," as he pointed to a pair of small, pointed muscles that looked like pyramids—one on each side of the midline at the bottom of the incision. I had never previously heard of the pyramidalis muscles.

The operation completed, we three doctors drank a quick coffee before the obstetrician commenced the long drive to his home. He had driven sixty kilometres, saved a baby's life, and was now to drive another sixty kilometres at two in the morning—and he would not receive a single cent for his trouble. Neither did my partner nor I receive any payment. Mabel was a public patient.

Each morning thereafter, Mabel and the baby were fine—but on the third day, the senior nurse, using forceps to remove the surgical dressing covering the surgical wound, changed my day. The masterly suture line that I had seen in the operating theatre was replaced by a deep gaping hole. To my horror, Mabel's intestines were clearly exposed. All but three of the obstetrician's beautiful stitches were gone. The wound was wide open, and Mabel's bowels were ready to pop out onto the bed upon the slightest cough.

I had never heard of a "burst abdomen," and the cause was then unknown. I would learn, years later, that the failure to heal was due to an invasion of the operation site by "golden staph," and it is the fear of all operating theatres today.

It was not a time for requesting specialist assistance, and I explained to Mabel that she must have another operation. I telephoned my partner, who left his patients in order to give the anaesthetic, and within an hour, we were back in the operating theatre.

My surgery was not like that done by the obstetrician. There were no pyramidalis muscles to identify, nothing fancy—just four wide, strong sutures through the skin, copious fat, and muscles on each side to hold everything together, plus some more through the skin. I peered anxiously at the wound each day, but Mabel and baby returned home about ten days later. Not a penny did she have to pay; again, everything was free.

The next two weeks passed without any major incidents in my life, and then came a non-urgent call for me to visit Mabel at her home. I pondered, as I drove to her home in mid-afternoon, whether it might be Mabel or the baby requiring help.

What I found was a black eye. Her husband had punched her. Was he refused conjugal rights? I don't know.

This consultation was in Mabel's home, so at last I could charge a fee—not a fortune, mind you, just eighteen shillings. Mabel would pay two shillings (20 cents), and the Miners' Federation sixteen shillings ($1.60), with the massive remuneration coming to me at a later visit to my surgery, not at the time of visiting her home.

Another fortnight passed, and having visited all of my patients in the hospital as well as seeing those who had telephoned asking for a home visit, I was having a quick coffee with my wife in the kitchen of my home at about ten fifteen prior to commencing my morning clinic. My secretary entered from the surgery saying, "Mabel Lesser is here, and she refuses to pay the two shillings or sign the claim form for the home visit. She says that there was no such visit."

Obviously, a punch causing a black eye is easily forgotten by some people. The woman had a live baby and her surgery (which would cost thousands of dollars today) had not cost her a penny, and yet she refused to pay me two shillings.

Philosophical and filled with kind thoughts, I was not.

I instructed my secretary to telephone every pharmacy in town to enquire whether I had written a prescription for Mabel on that day. Having confirmed that I had done so, she was to demand that Mabel pay two shillings and sign the form for payment by her fund. Washington Soul Pattinson replied in the affirmative.

I had operated upon her twice, visited her daily in hospital for two weeks, visited her in her home, supervised the progress of the infant daily for two weeks, and reviewed it on the home visit. Mabel paid and signed, with my total reward from her and the fund being eighteen shillings—less than the price of two cigarettes in today's currency. There must be easier ways to make a quid.

Re-Bore

"It is embarrassing, doctor. I wet my pants every time I cough. If I am walking along the street, I wonder whether people can see a wet mark on the back of my dress even though I wear a pad. If I am sitting on someone else's lounge and I cough or even laugh, I can feel a spurt of urine, and I dread that it will get through to the lounge.

"I saw a picture once of the back of a woman in America. She was walking along the street, and there were hundreds of flies sitting on the back of her shorts. Doctor, her clothes were not clean. Mine are, but the thought that it might happen to me frightens me, and I am starting to find excuses not to go far from my home. I am so ashamed, but as well as that, I have had three bladder infections this year, and I don't enjoy sex anymore."

Irene Murdoch was a lovely person and obviously distressed by her incontinence. She was forty-five years old, of small frame, and not overweight. She had borne four large babies to Jim, who was a friendly giant, and used condoms as contraception. Physical examination confirmed that she had a cystocoele as a result of childbirth. The circumference of the baby's head had been too large for Irene's tissues, which had been stretched and weakened, and recently had succumbed to normal intra-abdominal pressures.

The human bladder, male or female, is situated on the front wall of the pelvis and slowly fills to about 300 millilitres of urine before being emptied into a toilet or upon an ant's nest, the lawn, or whatever. The vagina is directly below the female bladder and separated from it by a very strong sheet of tissue known as the pubo-cervical fascia. The function of the fascia, with the assistance of some pelvic floor muscles, is to support the weight of the urine-filled bladder and other intra-abdominal/pelvic organs and keep them away from the vagina. It therefore is part of the floor of the pelvis.

Damage to the pubo-cervical fascia and the pelvic floor muscles during childbirth can lead to weakening and then lack of support beneath the bladder, which then sinks downwards onto the upper wall of the vagina, causing a bulge in its roof—no big deal, except that it causes the valve closing the bladder to be unstable so that a spurt of urine escapes when the poor lady coughs or sneezes. The cure obviously is to strengthen the pubo-cervical fascia so that it stops the bladder sagging onto the roof of the vagina.

"You have a weakness of the wall of your vagina due to having kids, Irene," I said. "But I can do an operation which should strengthen it and stop you wetting your pants and getting bladder infections—but I can't promise it."

"Oh! It would be better than winning the lottery" was her reply.

A few weeks later, I operated. The procedure basically involved cutting a strip out of the full length of the roof of Irene's vagina and then sewing the edges together whilst simultaneously pleating the pubo-cervical fascia above it into a strong cord to restore support of the bladder. Of course, this meant that the vagina had part of its roof removed and thrown into a bucket and was a considerably narrower tube than previously.

The last stitch having been put into the vagina's roof and the self-retaining speculum removed, I inserted my gloved right index and third fingers into the vagina to confirm that it was adequate in diameter to receive a smiling penis. To my concern, it was a little tighter than I had wished, and I regretted having put so much vaginal roof into the bucket.

I had heard army mates say, "It will stretch a mile before it tears an inch," so I comforted myself with, *Let's hope it is so.*

Before Irene left hospital, I said to her, "Irene, I want to see you in four weeks' time in my rooms, and there is to be no filthy business before then. Do you understand? I don't want that big bastard bursting you open."

The patient in the adjacent bed roared with laughter as Irene said, "Yes, doctor," with a laugh, mercifully unaccompanied by a spurt of urine for the first time in many years.

Four weeks later exactly, Irene told me with great sincerity how good it was to be free of the stress of incontinence, and she smiled when I told her that the scar was firm and that the honeymoon could start that night. I don't know how well Irene and Jim slept that night, but I slept poorly, as I feared Jim urgently knocking upon my door.

It was a few weeks before Jim came to me for some minor matter and greeted me with, "Thanks, Paul, for the job you did on Irene. Now she loves to screw and yips and yelps like a teenager. None of my mates knew that their wives could get a re-bore, and three of them will be sending their wives to you soon." Such is life!

Husbands Beware

Manny was a thirty-five-year-old female patient of mine. She was of average height and average intelligence, had a nice personality, and was always neatly dressed. She would consult me every few months for a check on her heart or whatever. She had no chronic diseases and was on no medication. She lived alone and was childless.

If Manny had a problem, it was a lack of self-confidence—it was written all over her face. The reason was that her husband, whom I had never met, had "flown the coop" some years previously. So Manny's life was to be alone while all of her friends had husbands. I could sense it as we talked, but that did not help.

There was a period of some months when Manny did not come to see me, and then there she was. As she came through my consulting room door, I could see a transformation: she had lost weight, her clothes were better, she had a new hairstyle, and for the first time in all of her visits to me, she was wearing make-up. She looked like a million dollars. She sat in the chair beside my desk as I closed the door and walked to my chair.

"You rotten little bugger, Manny. You're getting it, aren't you?" was my greeting.

She smiled, hung her head, looked at her hands (which were twisting a handkerchief in her lap), and said, "I told Freda that you would know."

So husbands beware! If your wife suddenly takes a greater interest in her personal appearance and looks sexier and younger, some gent may be giving his ferret a run in what you consider to be your exclusive burrow. Of course, the truth was that Manny at last had someone to talk to, to hold, to kiss, and to make her feel loved. Her physical appearance merely reflected her mental change, as is so with most of us.

Freda's husband, by the way, was a tough little coal miner whom I treated for broken ribs after the Miners' Picnic Day. He had volunteered to be a "Young Athaldo": to lie on his back with a large block of ice on his chest as another miner smashed the block with a single blow from a sledgehammer. It could have been worse; the other bloke could have used a mattock. But I guess someone would have intervened to stop the use of a mattock.

Tommy Calendar and the Giant

It was about 1958, and Tommy stood before me in my general practice consulting room, freshly showered and with clean clothes. He was as pretty as a honeymoon prick.

"Are you going soft, Tommy? I haven't stitched you up for months," I asked as I wrote him a certificate for diarrhoea. I was wondering what he would do or had done with his day off—he was too well dressed to be going fishing or rabbiting, so perhaps he was taking his wife somewhere. Perhaps he and his mates had already been on the mountain, moving silently in the predawn mist as they listened to the distant, mournful baying of their beagles.

"Aw, Paul, I'm keeping out of trouble, you see."

I liked Tommy, and he was definitely not a thug, a cheat, or a dunce; a nice bloke, I thought. Happily married with kids.

A few weeks after I had questioned him about his quiet lifestyle, he returned in a more familiar state. He had bark off the left side of his face and a two-centimetre cut above and into the eyebrow. Having procured the suture tray and carried out the usual scrubbing and donning of gloves, I spoke as I stitched.

"What happened, Tommy?"

"Aw, Paul, I was standing on my back steps, and the sheila next door was hanging some things on her clothes line when I yelled out to my greyhound, 'Get inside, you bloody bitch,' and her bloke jumped the fence and barrelled me."

I laughed and said, "Good story, Tommy. Try it on the cops."

But on another occasion, Tommy was definitely lucky when a giant neighbour knocked upon his door, a rifle concealed in a hessian bag. Tommy opened the door and the giant said, "Where's yer fucking kid? 'E thumped me son."

Tommy, recognising the content of the bag, promised to belt his kid, and the giant departed.

Sometime later, the giant, a patient of my partner's, was brought to hospital with a .22 bullet hole in the centre front of his chest and an exit wound just to the right of his spine at the back. The bullet had gone straight through his chest without hitting any major artery, vein, or organ except the lung, which had deflated. The treatment was a simple underwater drain, and home he went within a week. He claimed that he had accidentally shot himself.

A few years later, the giant left our town and took a job on a property out west. My partner said to me, "We should warn the police that that bloke will kill someone."

"We both think that he will kill someone, but he can't be jailed before he does" was my reply.

Some years passed, and the giant, having had a few drinks after a morning shooting wild pigs, wished to be driven by taxi to the property where he was employed. He approached a taxi driver who was playing tennis whilst awaiting a customer, but the taxi driver did not leave the tennis court quickly enough for the giant, who shot and killed the man. His defence was accidental discharge of the rifle, and he spent less than five years in jail.

Postscript

Many years later, when I was a specialist physician at Royal Newcastle Hospital, the giant was admitted to a surgical ward with eight or more .22 bullets in or through him. One had passed through his right eye and brain and then exited through his skull. He was discharged as good as gold about a fortnight later.

I have heard that he became a lovely man thereafter, which suggests, if true, that the bullet through his brain performed a frontal lobotomy. Too late for the taxi driver, though.

Come Urgently, Doctor

The following stories are told to hopefully entertain, to perhaps inform, and most importantly, to illustrate the need to impart accurate information when requesting urgent assistance. One or two of the stories are for trivial conditions and illustrate what nonsense doctors suffer at the hands of some people. Others are indeed major problems and are, fortunately, rare. They illustrate typical urgent calls to a general practitioner in a country town between 1954 and 1962.

I suspect that very few present-day general practitioners in Australia have similar working days to those of us in country practice fifty-plus years ago. However, all of these urgent calls about which I write, and far worse, are now routine to police, ambulance officers, firemen, and the staff of hospital emergency departments.

Crying Wolf

I had already had my initiation to so-called urgent calls that were a complete waste of my time, so my secretary knew better than to accept an urgent call without giving me the opportunity to speak with the caller first. I wanted to be sure that the request to leave the patients waiting in my reception and embark upon a wild car ride really did involve saving a life or easing great pain.

My partner's receptionist, however, did not know of my ruling concerning urgent calls. One day when my partner was absent, she accepted an urgent call from a woman who, it was claimed, was choking.

Driving quickly but not dangerously towards the patient's address, I wondered what might be choking her. A chop bone was a possibility in a gluttonous male, but the patient whom I was to see was said to be a not-so-young lady, and gulping down a chop bone would not be high on the list of possible causes. *Did she have heart failure and was choking for breath?* I wondered. *Who knows? Just get there quickly.*

Number 18 was on the right-hand side of the street, so I parked illegally facing in the wrong direction, grabbed my black bag, and ran to the front door—which was, surprisingly, unopened. I grasped the brass doorknocker, which was immediately jerked from my hand as the door was opened from the inside by a well-dressed, composed lady of middle age who said, "Mother is in the room to the left, doctor," as she extended her right arm towards a door.

Entering the room, I saw a sweet-faced septuagenarian in a white nightdress under a pink, lightweight dressing gown reclining upon a large bed.

"My arthritis is a bother," said the dear lady with a shy smile.

A short examination confirmed osteoarthritis but no evidence of a chop bone, heart failure, or choking. As I wrote the requested prescriptions, I said, "My message was that you were choking."

"Oh, we said that as we knew that otherwise, you might not arrive until after dark," said the daughter—who, it had been revealed, was visiting from a nearby town.

My smile was also sweet as I asked if they knew of the fairy tale about the boy who cried wolf.

It was decreed that the dear lady would never again cry wolf—as, six weeks later, she was found dead with one arm in the firewood box. I feel sad at the thought that this sweet senior citizen may have felt guilty because of my reference to crying wolf when the fault was clearly not hers but her daughter's.

Threatened

"A woman who does not belong to our practice wants you to urgently visit her son with an infected cut on his foot," said my receptionist.

The caller was transferred to me. She explained that her son had cut his foot upon broken glass some days previously, and there was redness around the cut and tenderness in the groin. I asked her to come to my surgery for a prescription for an antibiotic and some ointment and said that I would call on the boy in about three hours' time. She agreed, and within ten minutes she had the prescription. There was no charge, of course.

Half an hour later, the woman phoned again demanding an immediate visit. I had no alternative; I left my patients, who were no doubt inconvenienced by the delay, and was soon at the given address. The husband, a coal miner, told me that his wife had not returned home since leaving to collect the prescription, and he took me to see the patient.

The patient was about ten years old and was in bed reading comics. A small cut on one foot was infected, and some glands were palpable in his groin. I told the father to give him the antibiotic when his wife brought it home and to apply the ointment—exactly what I had told his wife to do.

As I left the house, I told the father that I'd had to leave five or six patients sitting in my waiting room while I came to see his kid, who did not need an urgent call. I also told him that I would not treat his family in future.

"Mate, if I call you, you had better come" was his threatening response.

My reply was simple: "Mister, I am not the fucking Water Board. You don't turn a tap on and I pop out. Just call your usual doctor in future."

I was on the footpath about to enter my car when he stated in a loud voice, "I'll mention you at the pit-top meeting on Monday."

Being blackballed by the Miners' Union meant saying goodbye to an income (no patients, no income, no future), and I did not need that situation.

Coal miners are good people, and it is very unlikely that a pit-top meeting—which would have included many miner patients/friends of mine—would have been swayed by this ratbag, who would have been well known to them. But I put my black bag down, stepped over the low fence onto his lawn, and walked up to this gent, who was, like me, not a giant.

"Mention me at pit-top and I'll beat you in seven different ways," I said, clearly in no mood for this man's threats.

A blue could have but did not occur. He turned and walked into the house.

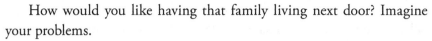

How would you like having that family living next door? Imagine your problems.

I heard no more of him, so my name was certainly not mentioned at a pit-top meeting.

A Gaping Hole

Most urgent calls are urgent, but some more so than others.

"You've fucked it up, Kev: you will live," I said as I stood in front of the patient.

I had just arrived after a very fast drive from my surgery. Kevin's distraught wife and a neighbour had been waiting at the gate to the typical miner's cottage and had directed me to the first bedroom on the right.

Kevin was sitting on a bed with his legs dangling towards the floor upon which lay a 12-gauge, side-by-side, double-barrel shotgun, both hammers closed over discharged cartridges. Two circular holes were close together in the ceiling, their rims as neat as if drilled.

He stared at me from a face covered in blood, his mouth a gaping hole because the front of his jaw had been blown away by the shotgun blast. His chest was covered in blood, but I noted with relief that there were no arterial spurts from anywhere in the sea of blood.

He was alive because the majority of shotguns are manufactured with 28-inch barrels, which are just too long to fit easily beneath the chin whilst the person attempting suicide holds the barrel in place with one hand and attempts to reach the shotgun trigger with the other.

The solution is to operate the trigger with the big toe of one foot, but fortunately Kevin had not thought of that. In order to get the barrel under his chin while holding the gun in front of him with a finger on the trigger, he'd had to tilt his head farther and farther backwards, which had the effect of moving his upper face and brain out of the line of fire. His first attempt at suicide blew away only the front of his lower jaw, and his second attempt increased the injury, but again his upper face and brain were spared.

The shotgun was no longer a danger, so I kicked it out of the way and called for the wife and clean towels as I prepared and gave an injection of morphine. My secretary had, upon my request as I departed on the urgent call, telephoned for an ambulance, and these gentlemen were soon dressing the wounds. I wrote a brief note to the doctors at Royal Newcastle Hospital stating that I had given Kevin morphine and that he had no known medical or psychiatric diseases. I then said some encouraging words to the anxious couple before the ambulance bore them away.

The diameter of a 12-gauge shotgun at the muzzle is not less than 18.53 millimetres, so we know that two cylindrical tracks (probably overlapping) were blown from under Kevin's chin through the bone and flesh of his lower jaw to exit through his lower lip. This meant that the amount of flesh of the lower lip destroyed was probably not much more than 18.53 millimetres—but I have described his mouth as "a gaping hole,"

Kevin's wound looked horrific, but muscle retraction had magnified the actual tissue damage. The reason for this is that a muscle encircling our mouth is responsible for forming our lips and controlling their movement, so when we pout our lips to kiss or whistle, we are contracting the multiple fibres of our *musculus orbicularis oris*. Kev's shotgun blast had removed at least 18.53 millimetres of this muscle. The muscle fibres then retracted, like a cut rubber band, to display a gaping hole.

Unbeknownst to me, Kevin would have the good fortune to fall under the surgical care of maxillofacial surgeon Brian Capper and orthopaedic surgeon Gordon Kerridge at Royal Newcastle Hospital. Both of those men were to later become good friends of mine.

It is unfortunate that I cannot show you before and after photographs, but I could scarcely believe my eyes when Kevin next attended my surgery. His gaping hole had become a normal mouth with only a faint midline vertical scar extending from his lip to under his new, perfectly sized and shaped chin, formed from bone taken from his pelvis. No beard was needed to disguise the surgery.

His hospital discharge summary indicated that he required no oral medication.

Having chatted for a while and undertaken a routine examination of heart and blood pressure, I said, "Kev, I remember the grouping of your shotgun. It was really good. The holes in the ceiling were small with no scatter around them. You wouldn't want to sell the gun, would you?"

His answer, "Get fucked," suggested that the gun was not for sale.

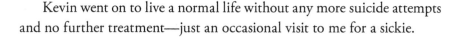

Kevin went on to live a normal life without any more suicide attempts and no further treatment—just an occasional visit to me for a sickie.

Call Me "Master"

It was about eight in the morning when John, a very caring schoolteacher patient of mine, confronted me as I was leaving home to visit my hospitalised patients.

"Paul," he said, "I need you to come see a colleague of mine. He tried to kill his wife by drowning her in the bath this morning. He believes that he is Jesus Christ and insists upon being addressed as 'Master.'"

This is the kind of call that every general practitioner dreads, and I said that he should get the man's usual doctor.

"Paul, we can't get his own doctor, as he hates all doctors and won't have the man near the house. You will have to attend without your black bag and anything indicating that you are a doctor."

John was a conscientious, honest person, and he pleaded with me to accompany him to the home of the man who had already tried to kill his wife that morning. His wife had been in the bath when he walked in, grasped her ankles, and, being excessively tall, lifted her legs, submerging her head. Somehow, she escaped drowning.

John also informed me that the person was over six feet tall (in excess of 180 centimetres) but that a third schoolteacher of similar height would be constantly present to protect me from violence.

It was clearly a case for the police, not a small general practitioner with or without a protector, but I stupidly agreed to follow John to the schoolteacher's abode.

Empty-handed, we walked onto the veranda and, without knocking, entered the hallway of the house—only to immediately be confronted by a tall, manic gentleman who said in a loud voice, "You were not invited to enter, so *get out!*"

Sheepishly, we turned and exited the home, only to be invited to enter. Turning again, we entered, and I was introduced as Paul, nothing else, no reason for being there, nothing. The manic gentleman was Fred. The third schoolteacher, my promised guardian, soon joined us, and he was certainly large. John, who had engineered my presence, quietly slipped out the door, and my protector and I were shown to high stools in the breakfast area. "Jesus Christ" left us and was noisily preparing for school as I admired the tasteful furnishings and the highly polished timber floor.

"I wish that I had worn my rubber-soled shoes" was an expression of my thoughts.

"Why?" asked my protector. "Are you going to run?"

"No," I replied. "If a fight breaks out, my leather-soled shoes will be slippery on these polished floors. I wear rubber-soled shoes if I anticipate a fight starting."

Patience was not one of my few virtues, and after five minutes of sitting like a galah on a perch, I got up as the manic gentleman entered the room.

"Fred, I must tell you that I am a doctor" was barely out of my mouth when he moved menacingly towards me raising his arms. I held up my right arm with the palm indicating "stop" and said, "I am a boxer, so if you start a fight, you will get one."

His reply did not raise my spirits: "It should be a good fight. I sparred with Joe Delaney."

The manic gentleman stood at least fifteen centimetres taller than me with arm length to match, so my only hope of beating him in a fight was if he had no knowledge of self-defence. Perhaps his height and belligerence had got him through life without anyone risking a fight and so denying him experience—at least, that was my prayer. But here he was saying that he had fought a professional. If it was so, then I was a candidate for a hospital bed or casket.

Fred's wife, whom I had not previously met, then appeared and said that Fred would be fine if only he could get some Largactil. I would rather write a prescription than cop a belting any day, so I soon retrieved my doctor's bag and wrote the prescription. All was quiet, and I fled the scene after promising to return in the afternoon. The offer was not refused.

There had been an unexpected delay of one hour in my daily routine, so I hurried to see my patients in hospital before commencing my morning clinic at ten o'clock. The clinic completed and lunch dealt with, I was again in my car seeing patients, including Fred, in their homes.

Tom Hosty, an estate agent, was having a bad day. He had unfortunately canvassed Fred's home with a door knock, and Fred had answered the door. Tom was distinctly frightened as Fred confronted him.

"Good morning, Tom. Good morning, Fred," said I as I walked up the front steps. Tom did not speak as he bolted for his car, and there was soon heard the squeal of tyres as he sought distant parts.

Fred and I exchanged pleasantries, and I was soon on my way without any commitment to return. Fred was taking Largactil, and I hoped that I had seen the last of this gent, who was another doctor's problem anyhow.

And so it was that my afternoon/evening clinic passed pleasantly, with nice patients telling me their problems and discussing life in general. Life was good.

An evening meal alone—my wife and children having eaten at an earlier time as my arrival was unpredictable—and back into my car I went to see the patients who had requested home visits. My equanimity was shaken when I read the list of patients to be visited and saw that Fred was amongst them.

"Well! He'll be last," I said to myself.

It was not long after ten o'clock when I knocked upon Fred's door.

"Good evening, Paul," said Fred as he stood back to let me enter. Having greeted him, I followed him into the lounge room where three people sat in individual lounge chairs: his wife, my protector, and another woman. Fred stood in front of a fourth. It was obvious that I was to sit upon an unoccupied chair, and I paused before it.

I did not see the punch that landed above my left eye and knocked me onto the lounge, and there was not a word or movement from the seated spectators. It was nothing to worry about—just Fred punching the doctor.

By reflex, without thinking, I bounced back up and was just as quickly punched down again. No cuts, no change in consciousness, just down I went. Fred had adopted a fighting stance, and so his arms were extended above and in front of me. I stood rapidly, grasped each wrist, and spoke some useless words. Fred went limp, and I stupidly released his wrists.

Fred threw a third right-hand punch, but I moved my head to the side, letting his fist pass harmlessly over my left shoulder, and put all my power into a left hook to his chin.

Whereas there had been silence from the onlookers as I was punched (my so-called protector apparently too frightened to come to my aid),

41

there were now loud cries of protest as the dispenser of violence became the recipient.

Fred spun to his left over an occasional table to land on the floor against the wall. I ran around the furniture and, bending over him with my right fist drawn back above his face, said, "Lie still, you bastard, or I will punch you through the floor."

Twenty minutes later, as the police took him to a psychiatric centre, he said, "Paul, from experience I know that they will let me out in three weeks' time, so I am telling you that I have two things to do when I return."

I had had enough of this gent. "What?" I asked in an unpleasant voice.

"I will kill my wife, and I will kill you." Having given his wife and me this comforting news, he left with the police.

I was not afraid of meeting him in daylight, but for months after that night, I would be apprehensive as I drove into my home after my evening visits to patients. I had a low hedge, and I was always expecting him to appear from behind it wielding a weapon. There was one certainty, however: he had never been in a boxing ring with Joe Delaney. A person skilful in the art of self-defence had not thrown those punches at my head. They were clumsy blows—but nonetheless, he was a killer if given the opportunity.

It gives me comfort to remember the small number of depressed people I have saved from suicide by saying, "Please don't commit suicide. Trust me—these tablets will change your life within the next three weeks. Please trust me." But this story, of the manic schoolteacher, does not bring me happy memories. The man was mentally ill, but from his own statement as he was taken away, he had insight into what was happening and what would happen. He had attempted to drown his wife earlier in the day; had assaulted me; and had threatened to kill his wife and me as soon as he was released. Why had he ceased Largactil? What a terrible life for the woman who had borne his children. What of his children? Was he a good teacher? I cannot believe that he would be a good influence on his pupils, but I am not a psychiatrist.

Addendum

More than thirty years after that unpleasant day in general practice when I was assaulted by the manic schoolteacher who thought he was Jesus and had tried to drown his wife, I was to again meet John—the sincere and righteous schoolteacher who had innocently brought me into that saga. John had risen in the ranks of teaching and moved to a school in Newcastle. I had retired from Royal Newcastle Hospital and had the relatively quiet life of a consultant physician in diabetes, practising in Newcastle.

John had developed diabetes and had previously been referred to me by his general practitioner, but the consultation about which I shall now write was quite unrelated to that disease. John, by chance, was my last patient for the day, and daylight had faded away as we sat in my office. My secretary had long since departed, so we were alone and untroubled by time or other people.

"Paul," said John, "I need a certificate to give me the next six weeks off teaching, and I am hoping that you can give it to me."

"Tell me about it," I replied.

John then told me a long and sad story of bullying and victimisation. His wife, whose only infant I had delivered many years earlier when I had been in general practice and whom I knew to be a nice person, was also a schoolteacher and had been teaching at the same school as John until recently.

The headmistress, a bully, had waged war upon John's wife and forced her transfer to another school. Now, having destroyed his wife, she had turned her attention to John. It was open warfare again, and she was apparently spreading the impression that mild-mannered John was a physical threat to her.

John said that he was concerned that his wife's mental state would soon be affected and that he himself had reached the end of his tether; the verbal attacks from the headmistress had demoralised him, and he could not face her anymore. He would be promoted to headmaster of his own school in six weeks' time and needed a certificate for that period only.

"John," I said, "I will give you the certificate if you wish, but it would be the worst possible thing that I could do for you. The headmistress has beaten your wife and is close to beating you. If I give you a certificate, she will point out to the other teachers that you are a weak person. She will destroy your credibility in the teaching profession, and furthermore, a certificate for emotional or psychological reasons will not look good on your employment record."

I added, "It would be far wiser to go back to school tomorrow and demonstrate to that woman and the other teachers that you cannot be cowed by her and that you are the best teacher at the school."

John stood to leave, tears running down his face. He said, "Thanks, Paul. That is what I will do."

I never saw John again, so I can only hope that my advice was helpful. He was a good man, and I hope that he had the courage to confront the bully.

Poisoning with Intent

Rats have been feared for centuries and it was no doubt a welcome event when a product containing Thallium, certain death to rats, was produced and readily available for sale in New South Wales during the 1950's. Unfortunately many people realised that it was a very simple method of terminating the life of a disliked relative or acquaintance and unexpected deaths occurred.

Aunty Thally

Aunty Thally, a benign-looking middle-aged lady, was much loved and admired by her companions, all of whom were female and living together—not a male in sight. A nun, you might think. No! She was a prisoner in Sydney's famous Long Bay Correctional Centre. She had knocked off four people with judicious doses of thallium and almost killed others (more, probably, than anyone will ever know). She was even found to be bringing thallium-laced homemade delicacies to one victim who was in hospital but dying too slowly for Aunty Thally's liking.

Her real name was Caroline Grills. The other prisoners had affectionately named her Aunty Thally. The year was 1953, my graduation year, and Sydney was becoming used to people being murdered with thallium. The source was Thall-rat, a rat poison readily available in shops, and the major symptom was sensory peripheral neuropathy, or very painful feet.

Less than a year previously, Yvonne Gladys Fletcher had been charged and convicted of murdering two husbands with thallium, and it was her neighbour's observation of the same symptoms in both of her dead husbands (including painful feet) that led to the exhumation of the bodies. She was sentenced to death but released in 1964.

The population of newspaper readers and radio listeners (there was no television in 1953) was subjected to more information on thallium poisoning and painful feet when my schoolboy friend—and later, international footballer—Bobby Lulham was poisoned with thallium. His mother-in-law, who had played "hide the sausage" with him, was charged but found not guilty of the poisoning. I have been told that years later, she killed herself—with thallium.

Bobby and I had been at Taree High School together, and he boxed at my home before catching the school bus to his hometown, Tuncurry. I was in my last year as a medical student when I spoke to him in Royal Prince Alfred Hospital in 1952. There was no treatment at that time for thallium poisoning, but Bobby had not received a lethal dose and recovered with temporary baldness.

There were others also charged, and so the population of New South Wales became well versed in the symptoms of thallium poisoning. Everyone knew it caused painful feet and later a loss of hair. Indeed, a blind man on a galloping horse could have made the diagnosis.

The widespread publicity in newspapers and radio about the painful feet associated with thallium poisoning makes it difficult to understand how a severely poisoned man could be misdiagnosed by doctors on five separate visits to three of Sydney's leading teaching hospitals, but it did occur. Five times, the man was sent away with the wrong diagnosis. It was August 1953, and the hospitals were Royal Prince Alfred Hospital, Sydney Hospital, and St Vincent's Hospital.

I had been a doctor for less than a year when I stood in the doorway of the small consulting room in the casualty department of Royal Prince Alfred Hospital on 31 August 1953 and called for the next patient, a Mr Lordan.

A large individual stood, then turned and picked up a small man from the seat beside him. The others present stared as the small man was carried, weeping, into my consulting room. I closed the door as the large man placed his crying friend into a chair facing my desk, and I returned to my seat. When I looked up, the small man still had tears running down his cheeks. Behind him, concealed from the crying man's gaze, the large friend pointed his right index finger at his own temple and made a circular motion.

Looking at the large man, I said, "I have never before seen a man permit himself to be carried, crying, in front of a roomful of people, and so I think that he has something wrong with him." Lordan, who had not seen the big man's twirling finger, did not understand my comment.

Turning to the patient, I said, "What is your problem, sir?"

"I can't stand the pains in my feet. I've had them for a week, and they are getting worse," he replied.

"When did you take the thallium?" I asked.

Lordan denied it. At my request, the large friend put him onto the examination couch and removed his shoes and socks. It was my intention to undertake a neurological examination of his legs at least, and so I commenced with a test of the plantar reflex, in which a blunt, pointed object is run along the soles of the patient's feet. The big toe moves as a result, either upward or downward, and which of the two ways is very important.

I never did get to see whether his big toe went up or down, as he screamed and pulled his foot away. Again I asked, "When did you take the thallium?"

Again he denied it, so I asked the large friend to leave the room and repeated the question. Lordan then told me that he had taken a full box of Thall-rat about a fortnight previously on a Tuesday, and so I ordered his admission to Royal Prince Alfred Hospital and continued to see the remaining patients.

Within about fifteen minutes, the medical registrar for that particular day came into my consulting room in some degree of concern, as it was his duty to admit the patient to Royal Prince Alfred Hospital. He had been given an outpatient record, not previously seen by me, indicating that Joseph Lordan had been examined at our casualty department less than a week previously. If my diagnosis was correct, thallium poisoning had been missed by the previous casualty doctor. The legal obligations and the adverse publicity for Royal Prince Alfred Hospital had already been recognised. Too bad for the doctor who had missed the diagnosis; I was confident of my diagnosis and said so.

Shortly, a policeman questioned me and then returned half an hour later saying, "Doc, the doctor in the ward says there is nothing wrong with Lordan."

"Well, constable, he can call it nothing if he wishes to, but it will kill Lordan in less than three weeks" was my reply.

Lordan died on 18 September, nineteen days later.

I was scheduled to give evidence at the coroner's court sometime in the future and was advised by a colleague of how I might be able to be paid five pounds for giving evidence. He told me that the five pounds was to reimburse a general practitioner for the time lost in attending court, and if I could trick the court into thinking that I was a general practitioner, I might be paid.

In those days, it was recognised that we junior doctors were learning our trade and that we should be grateful for a very small wage, as the hospital system was letting us use its facilities to learn the art of medicine. My salary in 1953 was, from memory, much less than ten pounds per week to support a wife and child, including paying the rent on a flat, and the only thing that we owned was a BSA Bantam 125 cc motorbike and some cheap furniture. It was not much to show at the age of twenty-nine, after nearly five years in the army and six years at university. The five pounds for attendance at the coroner's court would help, and all I had to do was give the court my home address and pray that it would be assumed that I was in private practice and not, as I was, an employee of the NSW government.

Wednesday, 9 December 1953, soon arrived, and I attended central court and gave my evidence. It was then that I learnt that Lordan had been misdiagnosed five times at three hospitals before I diagnosed him. The coroner complimented me on my diagnosis, and the Sydney newspapers had a field day, with headlines about a thallium poisoning case being turned away from three teaching hospitals.

There was a sad ending to the case. My cheque arrived, but it was not for five pounds—it was for one shilling and two pence, which equalled fourteen pence, the tram fare to and from Royal Prince Alfred Hospital to central court. I was poor but not so poor that I could not disrupt the government's banking system by not cashing the cheque, so I did not cash it. I kept it for many years but somehow lost it.

Occasionally, I wonder how many poisoned people have been buried with an incorrect diagnosis because a doctor had just not thought of poisoning. You will also wonder at the likelihood when I tell you of further mistakes in diagnosis.

The Fisher Family

Mr Fisher was sitting in bed, one of six on the enclosed veranda of the male medical ward at the local hospital. He had, after loss of confidence in his usual general practitioner, requested a home visit by me on the previous day. Instead, he had been seen by my assistant, who had admitted him to hospital with the diagnosis of alcoholic peripheral neuropathy, explaining that Mr Fisher's right hand hung, like a bag of lead, from his extended forearm.

Having introduced myself, I listened to his tale of a weakness in the hand starting a week or so ago. He explained that then, suddenly, he could not move it at all, although feeling was normal.

He was a retired coal miner, on a pension, living in the same house as his estranged wife, their son, and the son's wife and toddler. He did not smoke and was on no medications, and his hospitalisation would certainly reduce the takings of the Australia Hotel. Physical examination confirmed the presence of a motor peripheral neuropathy (affecting the nerves to the muscles), not a sensory type as seen in thallium poisoning (which produce pain or abnormal feelings in the nerves that normally carry sensations like touch, heat, cold, and pain).

I was surprised, however, not to see any of the signs of chronic alcoholism, such as flat swellings in front of each ear and extending downward over the jawbone (caused by hypertrophy of the parotid glands); enlarged breasts; spider-like fine veins on the skin of his chest; dusky red palms; a tremor of his other hand; or swollen legs. But I did see skin changes that I had never seen before. His arms displayed many dark greyish brown areas about as big as a pea with a flaky thickening of the skin, and I also found the same spots on his body. I had no idea what they were, but I knew that arsenic poisoning caused some strange skin changes, so immediately I put two and two together.

Having taken leave of the patient, I said to Sister Jones, "Have his hair and nails examined for arsenic, sister."

After we had walked a few paces, she said, "Are you joking, doctor? He is the town drunk."

The specimens had to be sent to a Sydney laboratory for analysis, and so I suffered a fortnight of snide hints about wasting healthcare money on useless tests. Then, one morning, as I was about to see Mr Fisher, I noted that the result of the tests had arrived.

"The tests on your nails and hair show that you have been given a bait, Mr Fisher," was my cheery greeting.

Everybody in town knew what "given a bait" was, and Mr Fisher merely commented, "That explains why I only feel well when I'm in jail for not paying maintenance to the missus."

A week or so passed, and Mr Fisher asked me if his married son could become a patient of mine, as he was being treated by "them idiots" for an ulcer and was getting worse, not better.

Of course, the son had also been poisoned with arsenic, and I reported that to the police. Inevitably, the toddler was then brought to me, and I honestly cannot remember what the child's tests showed, or even if I had any performed; but I do remember a conversation with a policeman. He was in my consulting room, the last patient having left.

"Paul," he said, "if you diagnose any more of the family with arsenic poisoning, please just treat them but don't tell us. You have caused enough trouble already."

Mrs Fisher was not the full quid and was the obvious culprit, but no one was ever charged, and the poisoning stopped. Mr Fisher's wrist drop recovered.

The source of the arsenic was an ant killer, widely procurable and called Deadant. It was meant to kill ants but it was just as efficient at killing humans. (A product available today for controlling ants and having a similar name does not contain arsenic.)

Many years after I left the town, a local informed me that a male named Fisher had shot his young wife dead with a shotgun and then killed himself. I have been unable to confirm the truth of this, but if true, it would suggest that the poisoner might have been the daughter-in-law and not the wife.

Stanley Jones

The long finger of chance moves strangely, and so, one afternoon, the brother of Sister Jones (the person who asked whether I was serious when I requested arsenic tests upon Mr Fisher) came to me as a patient. He informed me that he had been driving a busload of coal miners on an excursion to Sydney the previous day when he started seeing double. After leaving the city side of the Harbour Bridge, he noted that a street sign appeared double. The condition had lasted all day but passed off overnight.

He asked the cause, but I explained that there were too many patients in the waiting room (no appointments) for me to give adequate thought to his problem and arranged for him to leave and return, as the last patient, when I would have adequate time.

He returned, and the only added history was of indigestion and mild nausea. On physical examination, I found a healthy, fit coal miner with no sign of eye muscle weakness but the same skin changes as seen on Mr Fisher. An eye muscle is a lot smaller than an arm muscle, but it is a muscle, and he did have strange skin changes, so I sent him for routine investigations including arsenic poisoning.

A fortnight passed, and the results became available. Mr Jones returned, and I said, "The tests show definite arsenic poisoning, so we must now work out how it could have happened."

We talked about his job in the mine and whether arsenic was involved there or elsewhere. It seemed that he must have received it orally. I had him relate exactly where his lunch sandwiches were from the moment his wife gave them to him until he ate them. There seemed to be no one, other than his wife, who could be poisoning him. I told him this and elicited the fact that his wife had not left the grounds of their home for the past three months and had had no visitors. I also explained that I was not an expert on poisoning and that, if he agreed, I would refer him to a leading Sydney physician for a second opinion. He agreed and left.

Not surprisingly, he returned the next day saying, "I am sorry, Paul, but I am going to have to go to another doctor, as my wife says that I can see any doctor except you or a specialist."

Although it was fifty years ago, I can remember my reply: "Don't be a fool, Stan. You will wake up dead one morning."

Dr William Bye of Royal Prince Alfred Hospital had impressed me greatly during my time as a resident medical officer there, and I asked my secretary to make an appointment for Stan to be seen by Dr Bye in three weeks' time. Alas, Stan Jones returned to me saying that Dr Bye was on leave when he presented for the consultation, and he had been seen by a locum, who said that there was no evidence of arsenic poisoning and that his only problem was a stomach ulcer.

My reply was, "Stan, you might have a stomach ulcer, but stomach ulcers do not cause double vision, so that specialist is wrong. You have been poisoned with arsenic."

Two weeks later, I received an urgent message from the Sydney specialist saying that he had, as a precaution, taken hair and nail samples from the patient during the consultation, and the results showed levels much higher than those present when I had tested him. Obviously, Stan had been given another bait, and his life depended upon receiving no more.

I notified the police, who investigated the matter but made no charges. Their arrival, as with the Fisher family, resulted in a cessation of bait administration.

Stan is apparently still alive, as his name is listed in the telephone directory at the same address that I knew. I have not telephoned him, and I do not know of his marital situation. My call could not bring him happy memories.

Mr X

The wife of a senior person at a coal mine called me to her home at the mine one evening to see her very ill father. She told me that he was a widower living in his own home in an adjacent town and that he had a de facto living with him. For the past week or so, he'd had abdominal pains and diarrhoea that had not abated in spite of medication from a general practitioner.

The man, on physical examination, was dehydrated, delirious, and would, I felt certain, die within hours. There was nothing to indicate the cause of the diarrhoea, and the duration of the illness was too long for food poisoning.

He was transferred to hospital and intravenous fluids commenced, but he died overnight. Samples of his hair and nails were taken, upon my request, but the results would not be known for two weeks.

Naturally, I refused to issue a death certificate. Another GP, who was also the government medical officer, undertook a post-mortem before the poor man was delivered to an undertaker. I do not know whether he was buried or cremated.

I was not surprised when, some weeks later, the results of the man's assays (tests) arrived and were consistent with arsenic poisoning. I expected to be called to give evidence at the inquest, which I assumed would be in my town, as he died in our hospital. I was wrong in both assumptions.

Months later, the daughter—wife of the senior coal miner—came to me with a personal medical problem and told me of the sequel to her father's death. Within days of his funeral, a removal van arrived at the deceased's home, the furniture was taken, and the removal van and the de facto disappeared into the wide blue yonder.

The coroner's court was held, without my involvement, in the large town adjacent to the deceased's residence. The doctor who had been treating the diarrhoea was called to give evidence. When asked to comment upon the arsenic levels recorded in the hospital records of the night that I had admitted the man to hospital, the doctor claimed no experience in the interpretation of arsenic readings, and the coroner adjourned the court for lunch, during which time the doctor was to ascertain the significance of the readings. Upon returning to the witness box, the doctor stated that the levels were not abnormal.

So did a murderess escape?

It is my belief that our cemeteries must contain a number of people murdered by arsenic, thallium, or an overdose of a medication. My reasons are as follows:

- Doctors diagnosed Fletcher's two husbands as dying of natural causes, and it was a neighbour's suspicion of murder that led to their disinterment.
- In Sydney, Grills's (Aunty Thally's) victims were also misdiagnosed by a number of doctors and disinterred after burial.

- In Sydney, Lordan was misdiagnosed by at least five doctors before I diagnosed him. He died.
- Fisher Sr. was being treated for alcoholism when I proved arsenic poisoning in Cessnock. He lived.
- Fisher Jr. was being treated for a peptic ulcer when I diagnosed arsenic poisoning in Cessnock. He lived.
- Stanley Jones was misdiagnosed by a physician to whom I had referred him before tests showed further poisoning in Cessnock. He lived.
- Mr X was being treated for diarrhoea before I diagnosed arsenic poisoning in Kurri Kurri. He died.

So I proved poisoning in five people, with two of them dying. Ten doctors had made stupid diagnoses on those five patients. But that was between 1953 and 1962, and doctors are not so easily fooled today. You hope.

Poisoning by Accident

An unexpected death is never far away. Perhaps a carton of aspirin left near a toddler; ingesting the leaves of a shrub may kill the hapless man or beast [belladonna, green cestrum].

Deadly Cough Drops

An anxious mother carried her sleeping infant into my waiting room at about ten thirty one morning in 1960 or thereabouts.

"Can I see the doctor urgently?" she asked my receptionist, who quickly summoned me from my consulting room.

"I don't know what is wrong with my baby, but something is wrong," she told me as I approached. One quick glance at the infant in the mother's arms and I took them both to my consulting room, whereupon my previous patient was asked to leave.

The mother told me the story as I examined her child, and the diagnosis became apparent fairly quickly.

She told me that the infant had awakened as usual at seven o'clock. After a trip to the bathroom with the mother, the child had been dressed and left to her own devices whilst the mother prepared her two older children for school. All finished and breakfast eaten, the elder two departed for school, and the mother returned her attention to the youngest—who, over the next hour, became drowsy. The child was usually boisterous, so the alarmed mother sought help.

"Her pupils are constricted and do not change when I shine a torch into her eyes, so she has swallowed someone's medicine. Do you have any idea what it could be and when she could have taken it?" I asked.

The mother could not guess at the nature of the poison, but the time of ingestion could only have been between 7:30 a.m and 8:40 a.m.—two or more hours previously.

I took the mother, nursing the infant, to the hospital in my VW Beetle, and she then left in a taxi in order to question the older children, who were at school.

The child was normal apart from the constricted pupils and drowsiness, so no treatment other than observation of respirations, pulse, blood pressure, pupil size, and response to stimuli were required from the nurses at the hospital. I did not even think of gastric lavage, but other doctors might have undertaken it.

Although patients were waiting for me back at my rooms, it was important to await the arrival of the mother. When she came fifteen minutes later, her news fitted the clinical situation perfectly. An older child had said that she had seen the infant sucking a small bottle of cough drops. The mother had retrieved them for me.

The medication was a very powerful cough suppressant called Ticarda. I knew the adult dosage to be only fifteen drops. The infant had probably not consumed much, as the bottle contained a lot when I shook it, and the small bottle was designed to only release one drop at a time. I felt that respiratory failure could occur, but observation would indicate the need for artificial respiration.

With the mother and a nurse undertaking full-time observation, I returned to my consulting rooms. Six hours later, the nurse in charge telephoned. She said, "The child has shallow respirations, and the resident doctor has gone to the operating theatre to get instruments to do a tracheostomy."

"Don't let him operate," I insisted. "Just put an oxygen mask on her face and gently pump her chest up and down with your hand. I will be there within five minutes. Do you understand?"

The infant recovered after a few hours' use of a respirator.

Black Licorice—Too Much of a Good Thing

Many people have learnt that drinking coffee during the evening leads to a sleepless night. For that reason, my second wife (we had married in 1966) switched to herbal tea. She found the flavour marvellous and slept soundly as a result.

Ten years ago, to my great concern, we found upon a casual check of her blood pressure that it was 170/100 when it had always previously been 110/60. I immediately arranged for her to be checked by a cardiologist friend who confirmed the hypertension but found no other abnormalities upon physical examination. Subsequent investigations, which he organised, proved to be normal.

There had to be a reason for her blood pressure suddenly jumping from low to high, but with the investigations being normal, there seemed no alternative but to commence treatment. It did not make sense, and at lunch, prior to my wife seeing the cardiologist three hours later, I said, "It is all wrong. You must be taking something I don't know about."

Before she could answer, my glance fell onto a packet of licorice sitting on a shelf behind her.

"My God, you are not eating licorice, are you? It causes high blood pressure."

"No! That's a packet I bought yesterday, and it's unopened," she replied. "But I think my herbal tea contains licorice."

And so it was. Her herbal tea contained licorice, and she had liked it so much that she even stewed it in order to increase the flavour. The sudden large increase in her blood pressure had worried me considerably, and I had been fearing the presence of a rare tumour known to produce hypertension. But now, suddenly, it was apparent that there was nothing to fear, and the only treatment required was the suspension of the herbal tea.

Greatly relieved, I telephoned my colleague, saying, "Scratch the top weight. She has pseudohyperaldosteronism [pronounced *sue dough high purr al dough steer roan ism*] due to licorice."

"Was she eating licorice?" he asked incredulously.

"No! The licorice is in her herbal tea," I replied.

The diagnosis was proven by blood tests, and her blood pressure is now normal. She still drinks herbal tea, but not one containing black licorice.

Too much black licorice is poison for some people, but I do not know if it is possible to tell who will be affected by it or who can consume it with impunity. I cannot give you any scientific guidance about eating licorice, but what seems to be sensible, however, is as follows.

People consuming a lot of *black* licorice should have their blood pressure taken and, if raised, have a test for pseudohyperaldosteronism. It is a simple blood test arranged by your GP or hospital. Note that there is no need to have the blood test if your blood pressure is normal. People who are being treated for high blood pressure and who are eating or drinking a lot of licorice are in trouble, because the high blood pressure may be caused by the licorice, partly caused by the licorice, or totally unrelated to the licorice.

All of the people in the second category must see a doctor who understands the role of licorice in pseudohyperaldosteronism, as well as the use of the drugs in the treatment of high blood pressure, because suddenly suspending licorice or changing the dosage of the blood pressure tablets could result in serious complications.

I repeat: if you are eating or drinking a lot of licorice and are also being treated for high blood pressure, you must report it to your doctor and ask about pseudohyperaldosteronism. *Do not stop the licorice without asking your doctor.*

Quinine with Metoprolol

A common cause of hospitalisation today is prescription drug overdose or the interaction of two medications. A book could be, and probably has been, written on the subject, but just to show you how common it is, I will tell you of my own recent experience.

No longer a young man, I have developed occasional muscle cramps, which might occur in one foot or leg in bed at night. About a month ago, I had a really severe cramp—and as a result, I decided to take one quinine tablet every night to prevent any more cramps. Within four days, I was feeling lethargic and giddy upon arising from lying, sitting, or bending. I guessed that my blood pressure had dropped too low and found it to be so, at 110/54 on my blood pressure machine.

The possible causes of a sudden fall in blood pressure are multiple, including a "silent" heart attack, but I suspected that the quinine had exacerbated the effect of metoprolol I was taking for blood pressure. Going to Google is far easier than hunting through my medical books, and within ten minutes I found that quinine sulphate does increase the action of metoprolol and therefore was possibly, but not definitely, the cause of my sudden fall in blood pressure. They have ceased since another doctor advised me to continue the quinine, add Vitamin D and another medication for nocturnal cramps as I adjusted my metoprolol.

If I had dropped dead in early 2015, the sudden fall in blood pressure would have been secondary to a "silent" heart attack and not, as I currently believe, the result of quinine increasing the action of metoprolol. Of course, there might have been another unsuspected cause.

People are frequently dying from prescription drugs, including the interactions of different medication, so *be careful*. Ask your GP—and don't forget to look on Google.

In the Ring

The nearest my father ever came to using violence was when he jabbed his right elbow into the midriff of another, fleeter competitor to prevent being overtaken and to therefore win the Bangalow Handicap. The hapless opponent should have known better than to get close to Syd. He taught me many valuable things about life, including a love of the bush and boxing and good people.

One of his least important pronouncements concerning boxing was that a gentleman could always be distinguished from riff-raff when seated in the bleachers of the old Rushcutters Bay Stadium, as the gentleman carried a newspaper. The paper was not to swat flies; it was to be a long funnel to transport the gentleman's urine from his penis to the void below the rows of seats and so to the concrete floor beneath. Micturition through this paper tube was achieved silently and secretly, with the neighbouring gentry being unaware of the manoeuvre.

The riff-raff, however, were not so considerate and would point Percy in the general direction of the underlying void and release a deluge of beer-induced urine. The result was often the splashing of the riff-raff's own shoes and a deluge upon the exposed back of the individual seated in front and below him. Many a man, I imagine, would have received a wet back—and then a black eye for complaining.

Remembering my father's wisdom, I carried, as an impecunious medical student between 1947 and 1953, a newspaper to those same seats and for the same reason. When I became a doctor, I moved to ringside and no longer required a funnel. I could afford the better seating with easy access to the toilets.

On 12 April 1938, at the age of thirteen years, I had received a personal letter and manual of instructions on boxing from Hughie Dwyer, the retired undefeated light, welter, and middleweight champion of Australia. I retain them today. Since that time, I have done a bit of boxing in my own garage, the army, boxing gyms, university, and an occasional pub or the middle of a road. But, to tell you the truth, I could not knock a sick old lady off a pisspot. I have also been involved, in a small way, with boxers in Australia and England. I would like to tell you of some of them.

Brian Sams: The Fighting Coal Miner

At the age of twelve, Brian attended the newly formed Cessnock Police Boys Club and came under the tutelage of many dedicated men. By eighteen, he was already both a professional boxer and a coal miner. Employed as a clipper, he spent his shift hundreds of metres underground, pulling and pushing full or empty coal skips onto or off the continuously moving wire rope that connected every coalface to the shaft and lift.

When a miner stopped for crib, Brian would, although it was not his job, shovel coal into the miner's skip, as he reasoned that shovelling coal would strengthen his legs and body muscles but primarily those of his arms and shoulders. His aim was to have stronger arms and a harder punch but not gain so much weight that he would be forced to fight in a heavier division. This can be compared to Robert de Castella, Australia's world champion marathon runner, who undertook swimming as an alternative to running for training but ceased the swimming when he realised that his arms and shoulders were increasing in size, which meant more weight for his legs to carry in a marathon. Powerful legs and a light body and arms was Robert's desire. The reverse—powerful arms with a light body and legs—was Brian's wish.

Shift completed and having been hauled to the surface in a cage, Brian would shower before pedalling his bicycle a kilometre or two to his parents' home. Rested and refreshed, he would remount his bicycle to attend Claude Anlezark's gymnasium. Life was full and good.

Three days before fighting his first eight-rounder at Sydney Stadium (it was a Friday), he was working underground when he tripped as he passed through an airtight door and fell. Another miner then trod on his outstretched right hand. The skin was only grazed, and Brian thought nothing of the incident—until he awakened on the Saturday and realised that one knuckle was tender to the touch, and he would be in considerable pain if he punched anyone. Brian had worked and fought hard to reach the stage of being given an eight-round event at Sydney Stadium, and to cancel the bout sixty hours before the fight would be a death knell to his boxing career.

He came to me hoping that I had a magic wand that could be waved over the hand to rid him of the pain and permit him to fight upon the following Monday. Indeed, I did have a magic wand, and I arranged to meet him at Sydney Stadium at about seven thirty on the Monday evening. He would travel down with his manager early on the day, 14 July 1958, but as his manager did not wish to face the road trip late at night, he would return in my car. The main bout would be a rematch middleweight contest between American Al "Tiger" Williams and Australian Clive Stewart.

The shortcut from Cessnock to Sydney was, and still is, through Wollombi and Kulnura and includes an improved section of the convict-built Great North Road. It is mostly gravel with many bends but very picturesque. One feature that I admire is a hollow basin chipped into the eastern rock face about one metre above the ground. Even during severe droughts, it is filled with crystal clear spring water carried in a crack through the rock. It was the convicts' solution to thirst, as there are no creeks nearby. Aboriginal paintings are not uncommon in the mountain caves—there's one of a shark only fifty metres from the road.

VW dealer Kevin Tobey and I left Cessnock in my Volkswagen Beetle, and it was still daylight as I drove quickly but carefully along the gravel road. Coming out of an S bend, I found a truck, driven at the correct speed, facing me in the centre of the road with the driver unable to attempt to avoid a head-on collision. I took my Beetle into the narrow space between the truck and the rock face. Unfortunately, I could not avoid a large rock in line with my right front wheel, and we were stopped by a blowout. A slow driver, whom I had recently overtaken, passed us as Kevin changed the wheel. I can imagine the slow driver's comments to his passenger as he passed us.

Having parted with our money at the stadium entrance, Kevin and I walked down the wide corridor towards the ring and came, on our right, to the door to the boxers' dressing room. The security guard, at my request, put his head through the door and called for Brian Sams, who quickly joined us. Brian was perfectly relaxed and certainly not showing any nervousness at the prospect of fighting before many hundreds of people.

He took us to the male toilets, where he and I entered a cubicle and latched the door. After a look at his hand, I opened a small bag and removed an alcohol swab that I used to clean the skin around the knuckle. I then sterilised the top of a bottle of local anaesthetic before filling a sterile one-cubic-centimetre syringe and changing the needle for injection. The anaesthetic was then injected around the painful joint, and Brian was pain-free and ready to fight within minutes. His opponent would have a torrid time.

There was no sign of a painful hand as Brian fought and won his eight-round bout. Stewart, who later (at different times) became the Australian middleweight, light heavyweight, and heavyweight champion, beat the American for the second time.

Kevin drove us home with Brian sitting, somewhat worse for wear, in the back seat. We had experienced the start of a thunderstorm on our drive to Sydney, and as we were in the mountains south of Laguna, the damage left by it was apparent everywhere in the form of wet roads and fallen branches. Surprises seemed to be the order of the day. As Kevin drove out of a left-hand bend about forty kilometres south of Wollombi, a large fallen tree completely blocked the road. All wheels were locked as the car ploughed into the head branches; thankfully, the trunk was to our left.

"Would that be a tree?" I facetiously asked as my car came to rest amongst the branches.

We all left the car, pushing branches aside as we did so, while Brian complained of pain in his hand and started dry retching, which was understandable. He'd had a hard fight, his hand was painful, and he'd been confined in the backseat of a VW driven by a speedster on a dangerous road at night.

There was no serious damage to the car, and we were able to reverse out of the tree and then drive off the road onto the low bank and pass around it. What a wonderful car the Volkswagen Beetle was. Porsche designed it to suit Adolf Hitler's specific requirements in or around 1934.

Brian had a successful boxing record. He lost only one fight out of twenty-two and is today a happy man, proud of who he was and who he is.

Lionel Rose: Sweat and Tears

Nothing is more beautiful than the smiling face of an Australian Aboriginal child. Lionel Rose, one of Australia's best-loved sportsmen of all time, also had a lovely smiling face, but his opponents in the boxing ring never saw it. He was born on 21 June 1948 in Victoria and lived in a small Aboriginal community at Warragul throughout his boyhood.

His father supplemented the family income by professional tent boxing, so it was inevitable that Lionel would learn the art. He learnt it well, and at the age of fifteen, this boy became Australian amateur flyweight boxing champion. At the age of eighteen, in his twentieth professional fight, he became Australian bantamweight champion over the mandatory fifteen rounds. He was still growing, and his weight had forced him into the heavier bantamweight division.

Over the next thirteen months, he fought and won eight more fights and then a ninth when, on 11 December 1967, he defeated Rocky Gattelari with a thirteenth-round knockout. (Incidentally, Rocky's brother, ex-boxer Lucky Gattelari, is now in jail for his part in the murder of businessman Michael McGurk.)

Three months later, on 18 February 1968, nineteen years old and still fighting as a bantamweight, Rose achieved the unthinkable by defeating Fighting Harada for the world championship in Japan. A crowd of more than 100,000 people attended a public reception for him at Melbourne Town Hall upon his return to Australia. He was indeed a national hero, the first Australian Aborigine to win a world championship. But it was the man as much as his deeds that made Australians proud of him.

Having fought and won again in Melbourne, Rose returned to Japan to defend his title against another Japanese boxer, and then he defeated José Medel over ten rounds in August in America.

Back in America on 6 December 1968, he defeated a Mexican, Chucko Castillo, with the verdict not being well received by the Mexican element in the crowd. Rioting resulted in the referee and others ending up in hospital.

Rose successfully defended his world title and added the British Empire bantamweight champion title against Alan Rudkin in March 1969 before beating Ernie Cruz over ten rounds in Honolulu in June. I listened on the radio and was surprised at Rose's lack of impetus from the sixth round onwards but thought nothing of it at the time.

Ten weeks later, 22 August 1969, Rose defended his world titles in California, his opponent being Ruben Olivares. He was decisively beaten in the fifth round. Rose was no longer bantamweight champion of the world.

Having lost the bantamweight crown, he was immediately back in the ring but fighting as a featherweight. He won by a knockout in the fifth round against Garcia, his opponent. Five weeks later, Sotello beat him in the seventh round.

During one of these defeats, I heard the announcer yelling, "Rose is on the canvas screaming in pain, but he has not been hit." Hundreds of doctors listening to that announcer's words would have known immediately that Rose had been felled by a muscle spasm, a cramp. Many, like me, being cognizant of how boxers used sweating to help them get their weight to beneath the maximum level permitted for a particular weight division, would have realized that the muscle spasm was due to salt, potassium, and water deficiency as a result of pre-fight excessive sweating. It was obvious to me that Rose was being subjected to excessive sweating in order to lose weight before a fight.

A cause for his sudden loss of form was sought (the potassium and salt deficiency going unrecognised). During the following weeks, it was suggested that infected tonsils were the culprit, though I don't think surgery was undertaken. Next, a back problem was blamed. I awaited the certain announcement that someone had at last diagnosed Rose as suffering from an electrolyte (particularly potassium, magnesium, salt) imbalance. Then, to my amazement, I read that the cause had been found and that he was to undergo abdominal surgery for (from memory) an epigastric hernia. I had never heard such nonsense (although of course they do occur).

I wrote a long letter to Rose's manager and trainer, Jack Rennie, explaining that Rose's lethargy and muscle cramps were a direct result of dehydration and electrolyte imbalance brought on by pre-fight excessive sweating and fluid restriction in order to lose weight before the weigh-in. That I was correct was to become apparent when, within months, Rose was fighting as a featherweight and soon as a lightweight, seventeen pounds

(6.8 kg) heavier than when he fought Olivares. How much water, salt, and potassium had been extracted from his body in order to reach the weight limit for the Olivares fight? Poor Lionel had no hope of winning.

Before I received Jack Rennie's reply, I was able to read what Pat Farrell, sports journalist and God's gift to boxing, had to say about people like me offering their diagnoses to Rose. I could agree with some of his observations but rarely his interpretations or conclusions. He wrote in his newspaper column:

> It seems to me that, if anybody needs medical examination, malformities [sic] or abnormalities corrected, it may not be Lionel Rose, so much as the know-alls who orbit the Australian fight game.
>
> Frankly, I think that it has gone past the stage of mere irritation that we have to be told that Rose, a superb physical and fistic specimen when he wins, has more wonky parts than a two-bob watch when he loses.
>
> Since his defeat last week by Fernando Sotello, it has been discovered that Rose needs an operation to remove a blood clot from muscle tissue in his stomach.
>
> There is also talk that a small irksome bone may have to be taken from Rose's stomach but, as yet, it has not been made clinically clear whether this is one of Rose's own bones or a legacy from his last feed of fish.
>
> And, as I write today, Jack Rennie, Rose's manager, has in his possession a long letter from a NSW doctor, who, though he has never examined Rose, is quite certain that he knows what is the matter.
>
> The doctor, formerly an amateur boxer himself and a close follower of boxing and boxers for 25 years, has told Rennie that Rose has been fighting with an 'electrolyte imbalance'.
>
> The cardinal symptoms of this fearsome thing are lethargy, muscle weakness, muscle pain including abdominal cramps and backache, all of which may manifest suddenly.

The remainder of Farrell's article was four times as long as the above extract and consisted of his opinions and advice to Rose and readers— opinions and advice that made Pat Farrell the greatest know-all of "the know-alls who orbit the Australian fight game." He had not bothered to telephone me or another source to learn what constituted an electrolyte imbalance, what caused it, and how it could be responsible for the changes in Rose, and so he wrote a long newspaper article denouncing a condition well-known to many people but beyond his comprehension.

Jack Rennie's letter, dated 13 December 1969 was quite different. He wrote:

> I am most grateful for your interesting letter including your diagnosis of what you feel is wrong with Lionel Rose.
>
> Prior to receiving your letter, I have had Lionel undergo extensive X-rays by a leading Melbourne Specialist, Mr ---- of Collins Street, Melbourne. Mr ---- released the news this evening that he has discovered the cause of Lionel's complaint, which he states is a blood clot in the upper right rectus muscle.
>
> He has had other tests done such as a Barium meal and next week Lionel will undergo a kidney check, but it appears certain that this clot is the cause of the trouble for which we are very grateful.
>
> I intend showing your letter to our personal physician who may recommend that we show it to Mr ----, and I am sure that it will prove interesting and may have some bearing also on the discovery made by Mr ----.
>
> I am most appreciative of your interest in Lionel's welfare and your complete and thorough description of what you feel is his trouble, and I send grateful thanks from Lionel himself.
>
> Yours sincerely,
> Jack Rennie

Jack Rennie's penultimate paragraph indicates that he believed me but would, quite rightly, leave the decision to Rose's personal physician, who might then question the surgeon who planned to remove a blood clot. Their agreement with my diagnosis of Rose's symptoms as being caused by an electrolyte imbalance would have been an admission of the incorrectness of their own diagnoses of Rose, so I did not hold great hopes for headlines in the press. Rose was no longer asked to fight as a bantamweight, and that says all that is necessary. I doubt that the surgery proceeded but have no proof.

Rose did not perform spectacularly when fighting at heavier weights against bigger men, and there have been many suggestions of a lack of enthusiasm on his part and of alcohol involvement. My comment is that it is understandable that he had a lack of enthusiasm—just imagine how disillusioned and dispirited poor Lionel must have been during months of rigorous training, hours in sweat boxes, denial of a drink of water in spite of thirst for hours prior to the weigh-in, and all without result because, time and again, he was given useless advice and diagnoses.

How must he have felt when his muscles could not deliver the punch that they previously could? How he must have prayed for an explanation as to why he had changed from a punching machine to a punching bag? He did not know that potassium was necessary for muscle action and that his body's potassium was deficient because of excessive and repeated sweating—and that salt depletion and dehydration were also contributors.

What and whom can I believe? must have been his constant thought.

Lionel Rose, in spite of a mixed boxing performance in later years, remained a much-loved figure. He was a musician, and his songs were on the charts. He lived in comfort with his wife, the daughter of a former trainer. His friends, including Jack Rennie, remained by him, and he knew of the high esteem in which he was held by the Australian people and what a great role model he was to his race. He was named Australian of the Year in 1968.

I believe that my letter ended a short but sorry saga of poor advice—advice that could not have been remotely likely to be the cause of symptoms including "lying on the canvas screaming in pain, but he has not been hit." I wish that I'd had the honour of meeting him ... anywhere except in a boxing ring.

Pat Rafter: More Sweat

Yes, Pat Rafter is a tennis player, not a boxer, but his story is so similar to that of Lionel Rose that it must be told here. Tennis fans may already know that university tests showed him to lose twice as much perspiration per hour as other people, and you may have guessed that he, like Lionel, must have had an electrolyte imbalance.

I will tell you what little I know, for what it is worth.

Rafter was US Open champion twice and Wimbledon runner-up twice. He was playing and beating men like Sampras, Agassi, and Federer, and then in 2000 a disturbing feature developed. Like Rose, he was a dynamo at the beginning of his matches and was then felled by cramps.

That did not register with me, and indeed was unknown to me, until I saw a photograph of him at the end of a match. His long hair hung over his shoulders, and his face and body were covered in more perspiration than I had ever seen previously on any living creature, human or animal. My impression was, rightly or wrongly, that his hair was acting exactly the same as if it were a wet army blanket nailed to the top of his head, hanging over his back and weighing a ton. *No wonder he is sweating and losing fluid and electrolytes* was my thought.

Somehow I was able to telephone a person whom I believed to be his manager and introduce myself. I spoke of Lionel Rose and electrolyte imbalances and expressed the view that Pat Rafter had also been competing with an electrolyte disturbance. I pointed out that each training session would deplete his total body salt, potassium, and water—with only the latter being easily replenished—and that he would certainly have a resultant total body electrolyte imbalance. I attributed the excessive sweating to his long hair but could have been incorrect in that. The manager replied that others had wondered about the hair but did not say that an electrolyte imbalance had ever been suggested.

Following my telephone conversation, I had no knowledge of what subsequently transpired with Pat Rafter until I did research on the Internet for this article. I found that on 2 February 2001, Rafter had sweat tests performed that showed he was losing three litres of perspiration per hour—twice the normal amount. His long hair was discounted as a cause of the sweating, although I cannot envisage how this could have been scientifically proven without removing the long locks. Rafter is still deeply involved in tennis and the future of young players. I wonder if he has mastered the excessive sweating, and if so, by what means. I note his short hair nowadays, but that may not be relevant.

My duty having been performed, I forgot the matter until I decided to include his story for the benefit of the many others who, like Rafter and Rose, may be unknowingly suffering from an electrolyte deficiency. Perhaps it is superfluous as, more than a decade having passed, the condition is now well recognised by the public, athletes, and manufacturers of sports drinks and foods.

Sixty years ago, at university, I was taught that the people of English coal-mining towns were the greatest consumers of kippers. The miners working underground perspired excessively, and their bodies craved foods high in salt. Salt has been a major source of trade for centuries. Just enough salt is essential; too little prevents normal body function.

Al Burke: Wrong Diagnosis

Al Burke, ex-welterweight champion of Australia, was referred to me in 1975 to stabilise his diabetes prior to an elective removal of his gall bladder. The surgeon had heard from Al that on every occasion over the previous thirty years when either insulin or tablets had been prescribed for his diabetes, he felt awful. The surgeon was very concerned that a diabetic coma could ensue after surgery and delayed the operation until I had seen Al.

He attended our stabilisation course, and it was immediately apparent that he did not have diabetes, although his urine occasionally contained sugar. I broke the news to Al that he did not have, and had never had, diabetes. The sugar in his urine was because of a harmless error in his kidneys that permitted sugar to leave his blood at lower blood sugar concentrations than normal. No worries, and no treatment required.

My brother, Ian Lawson Moffitt, now deceased, was a true and naturally gifted writer—not a storyteller like me—and he wrote of this event in the *Bulletin* of 8 November 1975. The following is part of what he wrote:

"I was a shock puncher like Ali—I hit them fast coming in," says Al Burke, a former welterweight champion of Australia.

"And then one day—after I've won the title—this doctor says to me, 'You've got diabetes, this is the end of your career.'"

Bang! A medical KO or close to it: Burke gave up the game for a while after this body-blow. Then he climbed back into the ring, the shadow of death over him, as he fought Jack Carroll, Fred Henneberry; sailed overseas after a world title ...

"The doctors warned me that it could be dangerous," he confides. "A specialist in England even told me: 'You could drop dead in the ring.' And I never had diabetes at all; I never felt so good in my life when they told me that here a while ago."

Al Burke, who won his title in 1927, is a boxing success-story: a sixty-five-going-on-fifty with a map-of-Australia profile. "I'll fight the bloke with the big nose," the drunks used to shout when he was a star of Sharman's troupe. His real name is Al Pearce, and he is now a licensed bookmaker and respected citizen of Newcastle, NSW, where he whips up thousands of dollars for charity as a volunteer fundraiser. He is aiming for $4000 at present: his contribution in a unique fight to counter the growing scourge of diabetes in Australia.

Burke, of course, is more entertaining on boxing than he is on diabetes—ruefully praising Carroll, who took his title:

Old Jack used to chop the skin off you – he used to do things to you no other bugger did.

And Henneberry:

Carroll could only get nasty on you for a minute. Henneberry would hate you the whole fight.

He missed a chance at the world title, and jokes it was just as well—he might have been killed. And though he

71

refuses to blame the false-diabetes-shadow for blighting his career, he is pitching in now to minimise the effect on others.

Al, in short, is raffling a trip to New Zealand for two, with pocket money, to help support the Royal Newcastle Hospital's new Diabetic Education and Stabilisation Centre—the only one so far established in Australia. The centre has confirmed that Al merely has renal glycosuria, or sugar in the urine due to a kidney condition. The safety valve for sugar in his kidneys is low, so he passes it, but he is not diabetic.

So Al Burke is another boxer with a strange tale to tell. He was intermittently treated for thirty years for a serious disease that he didn't have before a surgeon referred him to me.

Allan Williams: The Quiet Performer

Allan Williams gave notice of what was to come when, in his first professional fight, he put his opponent to sleep in the second round and then, in his second bout, administered the sleeping pill in the third round. He had fifty-one fights and ended twenty-three via the shortcut. He became heavyweight champion of Australia and defended his title on numerous occasions. I was his second for his last two defences of the heavyweight championship of Australia.

Allan's manager was my friend Jimmy Johnson, who lived in Cessnock. He was a licenced bookmaker and owner-driver of a taxi, and he had numerous other productive enterprises. He was a good and loyal friend, generous and kind but endeavouring to give the opposite impression.

Jimmy, as a youth, had fought in the trenches during World War I and wanted no part of that life during World War II. He told me a little of his life in the trenches and that his solution, to avoid conscription in World War II, was to become a coal miner. And so he slaved as a coal miner during the war but resigned as soon as the Japanese surrendered. He told me that, when informed of the end of the war, he telephoned the coal-mine manager and said four words: "Scratch the top weight."

The manager, recognising Jimmy's voice, laughed and said, "OK, Jimmy."

He told me that, during the Depression, he and another unmarried gent took to the road as a team and secured work, near Singleton, digging drainage trenches. At the end of their first week, the foreman short-changed the wages by ten shillings each, a fortune in those days. When challenged, the foreman explained that they had an easy option: forget the ten shillings and have a job on the following Monday, or take the ten shillings and move on. They took the money.

Days later, stony broke, they were sitting in a culvert, protected from the rain by the road above their heads and warmed by a fire that had just cooked their final piece of mutton. The muddy creek gurgled in front of them. His contented friend, mutton fat running from the corners of his mouth, said, "I wonder what the poor people are doing."

Jimmy and I were sitting in the lounge of a hotel in Perth on the evening of 7 November 1959, having arrived with Allan only hours previously. Jimmy explained to me what the plans were, and to my amazement, he had me scheduled to accompany Allan while running the streets of Perth as light training at daybreak on the morrow.

"Cut it out, Jimmy," I protested. "I came to Perth to see it in a taxi, not on foot." But of course Jimmy won, and there I was, at dawn, running the streets of Perth with this giant, his back emblazoned with "Heavyweight Champion of Australia." A policeman on traffic duty gave us safe passage across a main road.

Showered and hungry, we sat with Jimmy at breakfast, and I was informed that Allan would be boxing before the press later in the morning. I expressed my desire to see him boxing, as I had not previously seen him in action.

"You will get the best look," said Jimmy. "You are boxing with him." And so it came to pass. Some hours later, in a boxing ring somewhere in Perth, Allan and I shadowboxed a few rounds—thankfully, without the press.

"I'll give you a black eye," Allan said in a matter-of-fact voice, and indeed it arrived just before the last seconds of the session.

Jimmy and I were in Allan's corner as he faced Steve Zoranich thirty-six hours later for fifteen rounds of hard fighting. Jimmy cared for Allan between rounds, but he was not a very good judge of points gained in each round; and so it was to me that, at the end of the twelfth round, Allan said, "What round was that, and how am I going?"

"It was the twelfth, and you are in front, but you must win every round from now on. You must keep hitting him, but don't let him get close to you," I said.

Both boxers had taken a lot of punishment, but Allan appeared to me to be more affected than Zoranich, and I feared that he would be knocked out if he got into a melee. Zoranich was much heavier than Allan also.

Allan fought the perfect fight for the next three rounds, scoring points from multiple punches but aiming to score points, not achieve a knockout. Zoranich did not launch an all-out assault, which surprised me, as he was behind on points.

The referee, Dinny Heaney, crowned Allan the victor.

There immediately appeared to be a minor dispute in Zoranich's corner. We were told, but I cannot confirm, that his seconds had differed in their reading of the fight and the advice given by them to Zoranich over the last three rounds. One had advised Zoranich that he was winning the fight and to fight carefully, while the other had advised him that he was behind on points and to attack in an attempt to achieve a knockout. The latter would have been the correct advice.

The *Sydney Morning Herald*, Column 8, was amused and printed the following:

REWARD. Dr Paul Moffitt of Cessnock, will be back on duty today with a new ailment of his own — a black eye.

Australian heavyweight boxing champion Allan Williams gave it to him.

Dr Moffitt, a boxing enthusiast, was sparring partner for Williams, who retained his title with a points win over Steve Zoranich in Perth last Monday night.

Dr Moffitt flew to Perth with Williams, boxed with him to sharpen his speed, and was in his corner during the bout.

And what does he get for it? A black eye.

OTHER CHAMPIONS

Another Australian heavyweight boxing champion, whom I knew well, confided in me about a period in his younger, wilder days. He told me that he had been a member of a racecourse gang which, having identified a punter with a fat wallet carried in his hip pocket, would use a razor blade to slit the bottom of the pocket and then follow the punter until the wallet, perhaps having been removed and returned to the pocket on a number of occasions as the punter placed bets, would fall to the ground.

There were two other heavyweight champions whom I met in rather unusual circumstances. The first of these gentlemen had been heavyweight champion of Australia and the other was to become a world heavyweight champion.

The first of these was Herb Narvo, who in 1947 gave me a boxing lesson in his gym. He had, two years previously, won the heavyweight championship by inducing dreamtime into his opponent within twenty-three seconds of the starting bell sounding. The poor recipient of his attack did not even have time to be afraid.

My memory is of his head, including headgear and mouthguard—barely visible between twelve ounce gloves—surmounting a huge, crouching frame. Even though it was only a boxing lesson, this was not, as he advanced towards me, a comforting sight.

The second short-term adversary was Joe Bugner, who had twice fought Muhammad Ali and became WBF world heavyweight champion in 1998. Fortunately for me, he and I were wearing dinner jackets, not boxing gloves, and were the two guest speakers at a Resident Medical Officers' Dinner on board the ex–Sydney Harbour ferry, South Steyne, which was moored in Newcastle Harbour after having been converted to a floating restaurant.

The dinner was the brainchild of some of the young doctors recently appointed in Newcastle, and its main purpose was to raise funds for the children's ward of John Hunter Hospital. One source of funds was a framed picture of Joe Bugner delivering a mighty blow to Muhammad Ali, and the bidding was vigorous. Of course, Joe Bugner was the attraction, and he was a master entertainer and gentleman.

In the chapter "Poisoning with Intent," I mention that fate moves in strange ways, as the brother of a nursing sister who had questioned my sanity in testing a patient for arsenic poisoning (which he turned out to have) also became a victim of attempted murder by arsenic.

Fate was again playing a part in my life as Joe Bugner and I performed on South Steyne. Elsewhere in this book, I describe watching HMAS *Melbourne*, Australia's famous aircraft carrier, pass majestically past me as I stood on the sands of Tangalooma whaling station little knowing that she would, in the future, slice through two accompanying warships on different occasions, sinking both vessels with great loss of life.

But fate had also determined, as I watched HMAS *Melbourne* pass by in 1962, that I would be a guest speaker in 1993 on South Steyne, which was also to become a victim of a collision with HMAS *Melbourne*. Fortunately, damage was minimal and there was no loss of life.

It is indeed a small world … or do I just move in strange circles?

Leaving Cessnock

The eight years of general practice in Cessnock were wonderful years, but I knew that I could not maintain such a frenetic pace for the rest of my working life. I just could not see myself running around from house to house by day and night, doing consultations in my rooms, and seeing patients in hospital for the next thirty years. I needed a fresh challenge; and so, at the age of thirty-eight, I decided to specialise as a physician. I was advised to go to the UK for training.

The Sense of Smell

I sold my practice in 1962, but my studies in London didn't commence till the following January. So, with time to kill, I accepted the position of medical officer at Tangalooma whaling station, and May 1962 saw me being ferried down the Brisbane River in a whaling ship to Tangalooma on the west coast of Moreton Island.

My arrival on this idyllic tropical island was marred by an overpowering, revolting smell that came from the factory processing the whales, and I immediately knew that I could not stay in that environment and would have to resign even before I had started the job. I did not resign, however, and I will tell you why.

Medicine speaks of us having "special senses." These are the senses that are attached to a specific organ: vision to the eye, hearing and balance to the ear, taste to the tongue, and smell to the nose. Our special senses are not essential to life, but they do improve our quality of life. Each day we experience many smells or aromas that do nothing to improve our chances of living through the day but which bring us comfort and happiness and are part of our daily life. But do not envy the florist who spends the day amongst fragrant blooms nor pity the resident living adjacent to an evil-smelling tannery. Their noses have lost the ability to recognise the ever-present aroma, or stench, of their surroundings.

The olfactory membranes responsible for the gift of being able to identify different smells are in each nostril, high on the roof at the very back. These membranes are made up of many millions of olfactory cells, and each cell gives off about one thousand cilia (three-micron-long hairs), which pierce the lining of the nose and wave like a forest of trees in the air we breathe. It is these fine hairs that detect smells and transmit the information, via the olfactory cells and then the olfactory nerves, to an extension of the brain. The brain then informs another part of the brain that your spouse is cooking scones or, in the presence of an odious assault upon your nostrils, that either your dog, reclining beneath the kitchen table, or the priest seated beside you has just farted. What a predicament! Do you kick the dog or the priest? Perhaps the priest, oblivious to the presence of the venting dog, may kick you first.

There are some important points that may interest you concerning your sense of smell. The first is that the olfactory cells (really their receptors), with some help from the brain, quickly adapt to the presence of an odour. Indeed, within one second, they lose some sensitivity to that odour and are completely unable to smell it at all within about an hour. This loss of sensitivity to any aroma is of great importance to all of us. Let me give you an example that you will recognise: a woman will apply her favourite perfume and rejoice in its aroma, but within an hour she is totally unable to detect its presence. Fortunately, others will detect it and perhaps murmur, "Chanel No. 5—so beautiful."

I once visited an elderly, retired, very well-bred gentleman who spent the majority of each day in his "office" with his adored, partly bald old dog. We spent an hour in his office, and I was nearly vomiting from the smell of his unwashed, ageing dog, but the air was pure to him because his olfactory membranes had long since lost their ability to recognise the nauseating smell of his much-loved companion.

A greater shock to my olfactory membranes came when, as mentioned above, I gazed upon the golden sands and sparkling blue water of

Tangalooma and was overpowered by the appalling stench that emanated from the factory beneath the flensing deck where a twelve-metre humpback whale was being expertly reduced to flesh and bone. All of the whale, except the baleen in its upper jaw (once destined for ladies' corsets), would be converted to pellets, as an initial stage in becoming animal feed. From the blubber, oil would be extracted for soap, margarine, or lamps.

I will have to resign was my immediate thought, but by the time I put my possessions into the small quarters allotted to me, the air was pure and aroma-free—or so my olfactory membranes informed my brain. My nose knew that the stench would make my life miserable, so it wisely lied to me and pretended that the stench had gone away.

The second interesting feature of our sense of smell is that repeated sniffing increases the appreciation of an odour in the short term, and so we "sniff the breeze" to clarify/identify an odoriferous presence.

Thirdly of importance is that the air stimulating the fine hairs of the olfactory membrane must be moving; motionless air will not activate the hairs. This is why, in the presence of a bad smell, you should hold your breath or pinch your nostrils closed. It is simple: no air movement, no smell.

Finally, the sense of smell in humans is primitive. Animals have a far superior sense of smell.

The olfactory nerves warrant a little more description, as they are currently the object of some important research into the treatment of paralysis caused by spinal injury or disease. Each olfactory cell gives off an extension towards the brain, and these extensions weave and blend together to form bundles that then combine to form the olfactory nerve. Just like the extension cord to your toaster or hot water jug, each olfactory nerve has a sheath encasing it, and the cells that form the sheath are, not unexpectedly, called *ensheathing cells*. It is these remarkable cells that hold such hope for paralysed people.

It has long been recognised that the ensheathing cells of the olfactory nerve have healing and regenerative powers and that they might be useful in healing injured spinal cords. Recently, British scientists/veterinarians conducted an experiment on thirty-four paralysed dogs (all paralysed by accident or disease; none was deliberately paralysed in order to be experimented upon). Olfactory ensheathing cells were taken from each dog's nose and increased in numbers by culturing. Two-thirds of the dogs were then injected, around their own injured spinal cord, with their own cultured ensheathing cells. The remaining one-third received only the suspension fluid without the ensheathing cells.

Six months later, many of the treated dogs had regained use of their hind legs, but none of the untreated had done so. Trials upon humans using their own ensheathing cells may hopefully be successful, and indeed it was announced in late 2014 that the procedure had been undertaken successfully on a paralysed man.

Cure of paralysis, if it ever becomes possible, will be too late for some young men whom I saw in Soweto in 1983. I had been invited to South Africa to deliver some lectures concerning the management of diabetes, and whilst there, I was offered a guided tour of the well-known and highly respected Soweto Hospital. (Nelson Mandela is probably Soweto's most famous son.) Naturally I accepted and was very impressed with the high standard of care and equipment.

All the patients I saw were black. Every case in intensive care was interesting. The first patient as I entered the ward was in his seventh day of treatment for tetanus. I was informed that he would make a complete recovery. I remember one middle-aged man who was clearly recovering from surgery. When I asked what surgery had been performed, the chief doctor replied in a casual way, "He came in at midnight with heart failure due to mitral stenosis, so he was given a pig valve. He will be OK." Unbelievable! A man dying from a deformed heart valve, caused thirty years previously by rheumatic fever, had been brought into a South African hospital in extremis and had been immediately given open-heart surgery that had saved his life.

But I digress. I should be writing of spinal injuries.

Another ward had some healthy-looking young men in wheelchairs. Intrigued, I asked, "What is wrong with these fellows?"

The reply staggered me. Their injury was not unusual in Soweto. Each, at separate times, had been seized by a group of men armed with a bicycle spoke—shortened, polished, and sharpened to a chisel point, with a small handle added. The victim had been held immobile by the attackers. I had personally performed many lumbar punctures for diagnostic reasons, so I knew what would have been done to the victim. His head would have been bent towards his knees and his curved spine exposed to the person with the sharpened bicycle spoke. The assailant would have felt for the depression between two spinal processes of adjacent lumbar vertebrae and slowly, carefully, pushed the bicycle spoke deeper and deeper into the young man's back until the spinal cord was cut. Paralysis and loss of sensation in the legs and lower body would have been instantaneous.

A high fence topped with barbed wire encircled the hospital. There was a single guarded entrance/exit, and each person was given a numbered disc by security upon entrance, to be surrendered at departure. I was informed that, prior to the installation of the fence and security, some wounded patients had been viciously attacked and even killed in their hospital bed by the same people who had inflicted the original injuries. I was under the impression that these injuries were tribal or gang-related and not associated with apartheid.

The miracle of ensheathing cells appears to have been confirmed by the recent successful reversal of paralysis in one man, and it is logical to believe that, in the near future, people with damaged spinal cords will be transported to specially trained neurosurgical units for harvesting, culturing, and injection of their own ensheathing cells into their damaged spinal cord.

Our sense of smell has been carefully designed, hasn't it?

Some weeks after arriving at the whaling station, olfactory nerves nicely dulled, I gazed out to sea as a large aircraft carrier, HMAS *Melbourne*, sailed majestically past after visiting Brisbane. I could not know that in the near future, she would, on two separate occasions, slice into and sink another friendly warship, with great loss of life on both ships—both tragedies the result of human error.

As described in this book, I, too, was almost wiped out by human error with HMAS *Ararat*. Nor did I know that within two years, I would, for the second time, be involved in a near collision of big ships at sea, again in broad daylight with perfect conditions, and again due to human error.

The London Years

The annual slaughter of whales had reduced their numbers to such a degree that the 1962 season was shortened due to the Tangalooma station being unable to reach its permitted quota and it ceased whaling. Following a short break, I arrived in a cold, miserable and smog-ridden London in December 1962.

Everyone Needs a Friend

London, 1964. The snow and cold of winter had passed; spring was with us, and our spirits rose with the change in our surroundings. The parks were seas of green from which burst a carpet of multicoloured native flowers. Brilliant blooms were in abundance in the gardens. But one seventeen-year-old youth was so troubled that he could not see the beauty of the world around him.

It was night, and I was in charge of the medical casualty department at Lewisham Hospital in London. A nurse spoke to me by telephone, saying, "Doctor has asked me to inform you that we have a young man unconscious from cyanide poisoning."

"Thanks, nurse. I'll be straight there," I replied.

Within two minutes, I stood in the doorway of the resuscitation area. Bright theatre lights illuminated the scene as two young doctors continued with their treatment of an unconscious young man lying on a surgical trolley. He was naked except for a towel over his lower abdomen. Dull blue patches could be seen on his glistening white skin. His respirations were rapid, and a mask was administering oxygen. An intravenous drip was connected to his right leg.

The bluish skin patches, despite adequate oxygen, were due to the cyanide stopping the body cell enzymes in those areas from using the oxygen. This is typical of cyanide poisoning and is called *histotoxic hypoxia*.

He will be dead within fifteen minutes, I thought. What I said was, "Have you phoned the Poisons Bureau?"

"Yes. They said to wash his stomach out using charcoal," said one of the doctors without looking up as he prepared an infusion flask.

"Fucking lot of good that will do. What else?"

"The book on poisoning says to give 10 cc of 3 per cent sodium nitrite followed by 50 cc of 25 per cent sodium thiosulphate over ten minutes, and we found a bottle of each, covered in dust, in the corner of that cupboard under the bench. I am just about to give the sodium nitrite," he replied. The other doctor was preparing the bottle of sodium thiosulphate.

They told me the facts as they worked. The patient was seventeen years old and living with his mother, who was separated from her French husband. They lived in a terrace, with the young man having a room on the ground floor. His mother's bedroom, to which she had retired after the evening meal, was on the first floor. Sometime after going to her bedroom, she heard strange noises from downstairs, and when she went to investigate she found her son unconscious.

He had left a note which, as it was attached to his admission record, I then read. He apologised for what he had done and wrote that his mother should not call for help, as he had taken cyanide, for which there was no treatment. He had obtained the cyanide from his science class at school.

The miracle did not happen quickly, but over the next hour we watched the youth's rapid breathing and pulse rate slowly return to normal, as did his blood pressure. Later, he awakened without any evidence of brain or other organ damage.

There were four physicians on the staff of Lewisham Hospital. My boss, one of the four, had been rostered on duty for that day, which meant that Paul, the patient, was under his care and that I would continue his management. The two doctors who had saved the young man's life were not part of my team and left at daybreak.

The relationship between the now fully conscious youth and myself was relaxed. We spoke in a friendly and natural way as the next three days passed. He was a personable, intelligent, sensitive, shy young man; indeed, he was what every parent would wish a son to be. I spoke to him frequently and at length, and it was apparent that he was not mentally ill.

I did not know what to do next. My boss, a physician and a very good man, did not interfere, and I was pleased when he agreed to request a consultation with a psychiatrist whom, I was hoping, would have a team of experts to manage this young man's future. Of course, I did not know that such a team only existed in a dream world.

The psychiatrist wrote in the young man's medical record that the

Australian (he did not even use my name or title) seemed to have achieved a rapport with the young man and that he, the psychiatrist, believed that the Australian could better manage the youth's future than anyone else. I was furious at what I incorrectly perceived to be the psychiatrist's lack of interest, but I now realise that he was wiser and more experienced than I. He made me responsible for the young man's future, and I could not walk away from it.

How could I, a stranger in that country, manage this youth's future? A week ago, he had attempted suicide. Could I just pitch him out of hospital to re-enter the despair that had brought him to me? I had about ten days to achieve whatever was possible, as then he would have to go home; but that ten days was enough for me to fill a vacant spot in his life, a spot that his father had previously filled.

When the time came for the young man to return to his home, I asked him to return one evening during the following week to visit me and my fellow doctors socially in our quarters. He appeared pleased at the invitation.

We had a small unserviced bar housing a keg of beer (no refrigeration needed in England), but no other drinks of any sort. It operated upon an honour system—if anyone pulled a beer, he or she signed a book, and we all paid our accounts as the keg approached empty and another keg was required. No doctor on duty ever drank alcohol to my knowledge, and I know of only one doctor who drank to excess. We would drink about three half-pints per person per night on two or three nights per week.

We doctors needed the relaxation and companionship of the bar, but an important feature was also the exchange of knowledge. We discussed the management of many medical matters and learned from each other (except Bassington, about whom I shall write later in "Saved by Being Learned Proper"). Most of us were planning to become specialists, and so our nights were spent reading medical books or attending lectures in other London hospitals. It was not an easy life.

The bar was a relaxed and friendly adult atmosphere to give Paul a feeling of belonging. He turned up on many subsequent occasions and was accepted by all of the doctors as a friend of mine. I doubt that many, if any, knew of his story as he mingled with us.

Fortune was with me in October 1964, and I passed the examination to become a member of the Royal College of Physicians of Edinburgh. I said goodbye to Paul and returned to Australia; but five years later, I was back in London on a study tour, and we had a pleasant meal together. He was twenty-two, single, employed in an occupation that he liked, and leading a happy and full life.

I have returned to London on several occasions since and have always checked his name and address in the telephone directory, but I have not contacted him, as I do not wish to remind him of an unhappy chapter in his life. I really would like to know what he made of his life, but I will just have to dream. What I do believe is that he would have brought happiness to others.

It is not only acquaintances of that great fictional Belgian detective Poirot who succumb to cyanide poisoning. It is still occurring in laboratories and industries today, as many people use it in their profession or trade. The treatment has changed, and kits are available (www.nohsc.gov.au).

Cyanide is widely used today in industry, fumigation, photographic compounds, silver polishes, and laboratories, and I wonder how many hospitals have the antidote. If you work with cyanide or near to someone using it, you would be wise to ascertain if the antidote is available. One of my diabetic patients told me last year that she was working with cyanide at a research laboratory in Newcastle and that her boss did not share her concerns about safety, with resultant friction between the two.

A colleague of mine was working in a laboratory three or so years ago in a leading Sydney hospital, and having finished his work with liquid cyanide (which is harmless if you do not drink it), he emptied it into a laboratory sink. He was unfortunate on this day, because earlier another researcher had discarded acid into the sink, and that acid turned the liquid cyanide into hydrocyanic acid—a gas that my friend inhaled. He recognised the smell of almonds, instantly realised that he was in trouble, and announced the diagnosis and treatment as he made a precipitous arrival at the casualty department.

Cyanide also occurs naturally in plants as amygdalin, which releases cyanide if ingested. One of these plants is cassava, but the quantity of cyanide in cassava is so small that nobody is poisoned. There are at least two types of cassava growing in India; one, which is the nicer, does not have cyanide, whereas the cheaper and less pleasant one does. I was told that rodents don't like the cheaper one and avoid eating it in the fields. It has been suggested that the cyanide in cassava might cause a form of diabetes that only occurs in India.

Saved by Being Learned Proper

Lewisham and its neighbouring suburb, Blackheath, are in South East London. With the Thames nearby, it is a middle-class suburb with lovely parks and gardens and charmingly typical English pubs where nice people meet, accompanied by their dogs, some of whom also quite like English beer.

I was one of fifty-seven doctors who applied for the position of medical registrar at Lewisham Hospital. Having survived a very severe grilling by a London medical board, whose members seemed to think that I was the Antipodes' answer to Jack the Ripper, I commenced duties in January 1964.

It was a general hospital for medicine, surgery, orthopaedics, paediatrics, obstetrics and gynaecology, emergencies, and outpatient clinics. The specialists were all English, and as one would expect, they were very capable and held in high esteem. They lived in the community, but the rest of us lived at the hospital.

The rank below the specialists was my rank of registrar, and we came from Britain or the Commonwealth in a ratio of about 60:40. Below the registrars were the senior and junior resident medical officers, who came from Britain and many other countries in the same ratio. My reason for being there was to try to learn enough about medicine to succeed at one of the specialist examinations held in London and Edinburgh. It was well known that about four hundred doctors would offer themselves as candidates at each examination but that only 16 per cent would pass the exam. It was, therefore, highly competitive, and the devil took not just the hindmost but 84 per cent.

Another registrar was Bassington, said to be Irish but more English than the English with his Savile Row suits, cultured voice, upper-class mannerisms, and the persona of a Mafia don. His aim was, as with many of us, to become a specialist. He and I could have helped each other by intelligent discussion of medical matters, but I quickly realised that

Bassington treated a discussion as a debate that he had to win, and his information was therefore unreliable.

He would manufacture facts just to win a point, and his favourite ploy, when challenged, was to say, "Have you read the latest edition of Harrison [or some other textbook]?" Of course, he was implying that the other person's information was outdated. Repeating Bassington's words of wisdom to an examiner would be an act of suicide, so I avoided medical discussions with him. In life and especially in medical examinations, incomplete knowledge of a subject is preferable to incorrect knowledge, so it is wise to avoid a person known to be economical with the truth or only interested in scoring points.

The food served to the doctors was not good. If you did not like mashed potatoes, you would starve, as it was the only food available in large quantities. Saturday night's meal was the worst of all, as the kitchen staff finished work at four in the afternoon and left our food in a warmer until served at seven o'clock. Can you imagine a dinner of two fried eggs, potato chips, and whatever—cabbage, probably—kept for three hours in a warmer? There would have been ice cream and tinned peaches, I suppose, but I cannot remember. The patients ate better.

We avoided that meal in a number of ways, with one method being for us all to contribute, every three or four months, to hiring a caterer. Lounge suits and ties were compulsory, or the person's national costume. No operating gowns were allowed.

On one of these occasions, the tables had been brought together to form one long table covered with starched tablecloths. Thirty or so men and women were eating by candlelight, with the national dress of the women adding marvellous colour to the scene. Half of the faces were white, being English, Irish (Bassington), and Australian (me and another male doctor on a two-week stint), with the remainder of the diners from Ghana, Nigeria, India, Pakistan, Burma, Malaya, and Jamaica. A more friendly group of people could not be imagined—but alas! Bassington was there.

We were eating jugged hare when I heard Bassington, who was seated at the head of the table near the recently arrived Australian, give an erudite opinion upon Australian accents in a voice deliberately loud enough to entice me into debate. The jugged hare was more important, and I ignored the bait; but soon one of my English friends said in a loud voice, heard by everyone at the table, "Paul, Bassington says that he can tell from an Australian's accent which Australian state the person comes from. What do you think of that?"

Everybody in the room had a different accent, so my reply interested everyone. All conversation ceased, and the people at the long table listened to my reply.

"I accept that people from different social classes vary in accent in Australia and some words, such as *Newcastle*, are pronounced differently in certain areas, but I do not think that there is an accent identifiable with any particular state."

All remained quiet as Bassington, the born debater, gave lengthy proof of how little I knew on the subject of my own country and our accent—and then, carried away with his own eloquence and self-importance, unwittingly handed me a gift from heaven. I could not believe my luck as he finished his long dissertation with the words, "So don't tell me that each state doesn't speak different."

I picked up my knife and fork and, without taking my eyes from my plate, said one word only.

"Different ... *ly*," emphasising the *ly*.

The room erupted in shouts of "touché," cheers, and loud stamping of the English doctors' feet. They loved it, and my Commonwealth friends' black, yellow, or red faces were beaming as they realised that somehow or other the friendly Australian had beaten the arrogant Bassington by saying one word only.

My jugged hare seemed to take on a new special delicacy. The candles seemed to glow more brightly, but not as brightly as Bassington's face in its shades of red and purple.

One up for the convict country. It had learned me proper.

Doctor at Sea

T he foghorn blared forlornly above my head as MV *Melbourne Star* slowly made her way down the Thames at night in October 1964. I had spent the previous two years studying and working in London hospitals in order to improve my medical skills to a degree sufficient to pass the examination to qualify as a member of either the London or Edinburgh College of Physicians. At last, I had been successful, and I could return to Australia with a specialist degree. It had been twelve years since I had graduated as a doctor.

The two years in the United Kingdom had been expensive, and I was being as frugal as possible, so I avoided the airfare back to Australia by taking a job as ship's doctor from London to Sydney. Rather than borrow hundreds of dollars for my airfare, I would be paid to return to Australia. But it was not the decision of a financial genius, as the trip would take about six to eight weeks, and the pay was a mere one shilling—which I was never paid anyhow. I avoided the airfare but was eight weeks unpaid. Not clever, perhaps, but I am pleased that I did it, because the trip was marvellous.

How different were my thoughts, as the foghorn blared, to those of the crew of the original MV *Melbourne Star*, who a mere twenty-two years previously had sailed in company with thirteen other merchant ships in Operation Pedestal, attempting to bring supplies, fuel, and munitions to Malta as World War II was at it blackest. Malta, a small island in the Mediterranean, was essential in the Allied efforts to stop the German and Italian armies in North Africa from receiving fuel and supplies, but Malta itself required fuel and supplies, two previous convoys having failed to reach it.

MV *Melbourne Star* and the other merchant vessels in the convoy were protected by a vast allied fleet—including two battleships, five aircraft carriers, seven light cruisers, twenty-seven destroyers, three fleet oilers, and a rescue tug—as they entered the Mediterranean on 9 August 1942. MV *Melbourne Star* and four other vessels were the only merchant ships to survive the Axis naval and air attacks. Nine merchant ships, one aircraft carrier, two cruisers, and one destroyer had been sunk. *Brisbane Star* arrived a day after *Melbourne Star* with its bow blown off by a torpedo. The fifth and last surviving merchant ship arrived a day later, held upright by other ships fastened to its sides.

Those *Melbourne Star* sailors who had lived through the Axis onslaught had little longer to live, however, as seven months later MV *Melbourne Star* was sunk near Bermuda by a torpedo from a German submarine. There were only four survivors from a crew of 117, and they then drifted in a lifeboat for thirty-nine days before being sighted and rescued. I wonder if any of the four sailors survived the following three years of sailing seas plagued by submarines, ships, mines, and planes deployed to sink Allied ships.

The Blue Star Line had forty-one ships when the war broke out, but twenty-nine were destroyed during the next six years. *Brisbane Star*, with repairs to her bow, was one of the twelve ships fortunate enough to still be afloat at war's end. What a life, and what a way to die. What courage those sailors showed! They lived each day in fear of death but believing that their small contribution to protecting the lives of their loved ones was their duty.

The MV *Melbourne Star* bearing me home to Australia had been built in1947 as a result of the previous MV *Melbourne Star's* sinking and was, I thought, a big ship at 165 metres. She was a refrigerated merchant vessel carrying perishables—but, as a sideline, she had accommodation for twelve passengers, including the compulsory ship's doctor. She also had a deck cargo. Horses occasionally stared at me from dark stables, and a large hound on a lead would grace the deck accompanied by a gold-braided young officer. As I watched, I could not help but think that the officer did not like the ignominy of leading a dog and gave the impression that the task was beneath his dignity; he should be guiding a big ship, not a dog. Neither the dog nor I was aware of future events involving the guidance of this big ship.

My fellow passengers were a mixed bunch, with the most noteworthy being a small, obese Frenchwoman who carried large scissors in her handbag during the German occupation of France. She did not claim to have stabbed anyone, but my assessment of her was that mentally and physically, she was certainly capable of being the survivor in a physical contest, in spite of her small height and rotund shape. She enjoyed deck tennis and would laugh uproariously as she had me running madly around my side of the court. Each day carried us further away from the English winter, and shortly, we were pleased to see a very large canvas swimming pool erected on the afterdeck.

The Caribbean was a very different picture to what we had experienced in the Atlantic. Gone were the dark skies and the dull green water. Now we had bright sun, sparkling blue ocean, and cloudless skies. Our skin was warm and our personalities brighter. There was nothing to suggest that five kilometres beneath the tranquil surface lay the Cayman Trough, a deep valley in the sea floor formed by the junction of tectonic plates incorporating a number of fault zones. The trough is home to active volcanoes that spew their superheated contents into the surrounding ocean—a peaceful surface above concealing a hot and violent world below.

A lazy, sunny morning having passed, the passengers and I joined the captain for lunch. The atmosphere was relaxed as we spoke of passing through the Panama Canal. One of the joys of being aboard that ship was the quiet, the throb of the motors being the only sound apart from an occasional gull. But suddenly, our peace was shattered by two blasts from a foghorn, which were immediately answered by a blast from directly above us. The captain jumped up, sending his chair flying backwards, as the first blasts occurred and ran up the staircase to the deck above.

Bewildered, we passengers left our meals and walked to the port side from where the two blasts had emanated. To our amazement and horror, we saw another large ship less than fifty metres from us and running at an angle towards us. The blast from our ship's foghorn had indicated "I am turning to starboard," and the double blast from the other ship indicated "I am turning to port." But the other ship appeared to be getting closer before it became apparent that a collision of the two very large ships would not occur. None of us returned to the table.

How could that happen in broad daylight with clear visibility and a smooth sea? Well! I have no knowledge of the true circumstances, but I believe that, firstly, each ship was on automatic pilot. Secondly, the ships were sailing intersecting courses that would have brought them into a sideways collision. Perhaps the gold-braided young officer may have been in charge. Perhaps the dog had got his paws on the wheel.

The truth is that the sea, just like our roads, has a right of way dictating which ship must give way to the other, and the *International Regulations for Preventing Collisions at Sea* includes the saying, "If to starboard red appear, 'tis your duty to keep clear." This, if applicable in our case, indicates that it was the responsibility of the other ship to avoid colliding with MV *Melbourne Star* and that neither our officer nor the dog was to blame.

Life was soon back to normal, and the swimming pool was in constant use—although it brought disaster to a mid-thirties mother who fractured her ankle when she slipped. It was a simple break, and I merely had to plaster the foot, ankle, and a little way up the leg. I then forgot about it, but it was not finished with me.

Colón is a city at the eastern end of the Panama Canal, with Panama being to the west, and it was with great anticipation that we awaited our arrival there. My joy was to be short-lived, however, as I was informed that it was routine for patients with fractures treated on board to be reviewed by a shore-based doctor. My patient and I would be off-loaded at Colón in order for X-rays to be taken. The GP, to whom we were taken in a taxi, quickly took an X-ray, and we were back in a taxi for a night ride to Panama. I was disappointed and angry; indeed, I am still angry. I had been denied the opportunity to see the Panama Canal. Surely I must be the only ship's doctor in the world to have sailed the Panama Canal in a taxi. Did I see the Panama Canal? No.

The ceremony of initiation for those of us who were crossing the equator on a ship for the first time was good fun—and, of course, we were sailing into summer, so each day was warm. Flying fish would somehow deposit themselves on our decks high above the sea, and dolphins were permanently stationed one metre in front of our bow, effortlessly leading us home.

Finally, I was back in Australia and back in Cessnock, employed immediately, if temporarily, as a locum for my former partner in general practice. The reason was a sad one. A pregnant woman had called at his surgery two days previously for a routine, uncomplicated prenatal visit:

weighing, urine testing, blood pressure, abdominal palpation, etc. Seeing that she would have to wait half an hour or so, she asked the receptionist to have the doctor come to her home that evening instead. She lived fifteen kilometres away but did not think it unreasonable to ask the doctor to undertake a thirty-kilometre round trip to see her at her home rather than wait thirty minutes to see him in his surgery.

He was an exceptional man—always calm and only seeing good. His life's purpose was to help people. He'd had little sleep the previous night, as he had stayed at the bedside of a dying patient in order to comfort the distressed wife and to permit the dying man to die quietly in his own home. Having completed his afternoon clinic and eaten his evening meal, he commenced his home calls, including the thirty-kilometre round trip to the non-urgent pregnant woman.

He fell asleep at the wheel of his car when returning to his home, hit a kerbside tree, became paralysed by a fractured neck, and died in hospital months later, leaving a widow and young children. The pregnant woman's selfishness was largely responsible for his death and forever changed the lives of his wife and children.

The sea is a dangerous place, but so is the land—and often it is another person who thoughtlessly, on sea or land, makes it so.

Up There for Thinking

We have all been impressed by the amazing brain function of some people. A good example of an exceptional brain would have to be a man you know as Professor Gus Nossal.

Gus was the younger brother of my younger brother Ian's best friend and was one year behind me in medical school at the University of Sydney. The time was January 1953, and I, having completed the six years of medicine and being employed at Royal Prince Alfred Hospital, made a shortcut through the University of Sydney grounds and stopped to read, upon a noticeboard, the results of the recently completed fifth-year examinations.

There were in excess of two hundred medical students attempting four different subjects—perhaps more, I forget. What I am sure of, though, is that Gus Nossal's name headed the list in every subject but one. Somehow or other, another candidate had beaten him into second place in one subject. Some wag, undoubtedly with racehorses in his blood, had used a biro to encircle Gus's name in second position and scrawl "Swabbed" beside it. Obviously, the wag believed that nobody could beat Gus unless he had been doped.

Many people's thinking skills have impressed me during my lifetime, but two had unusual solutions to their specific problem. Perhaps these gentlemen were "lateral thinkers" rather than geniuses (like Nossal), but they certainly thought and planned, and their ingenuity is worth recording.

Fooling the Taxman

The first gentleman was Solan, a thirty-five-year-old Greek who, when I met him in 1963, owned a restaurant in London. He was of ideal height and weight, handsome and with a lovely nature. He was indeed an Adonis, although I did not recognise that at the time. His wife, who rarely came to the restaurant, could easily have played the role of Aphrodite; she was dark, slim, beautiful, and aloof. They had an eight-year-old daughter whom I never met.

Having graduated in medicine a decade previously, I was in London endeavouring to learn enough to convince examiners that I should be classed as a specialist, and such a task involved long hours of study and my attendance at many London hospitals. At one stage, I required accommodation in close proximity to the major hospitals, and I rented a room above Solan's restaurant—with the result that he and I occasionally sat in his restaurant drinking coffee after the last customers had left.

He told me of his arrival in London from Greece with a suitcase and two shillings. Leaving his suitcase in temporary storage, he walked from restaurant to restaurant until he found a job; the following day, he commenced washing dishes. Within two weeks, he had two dishwashing jobs, the second in the evening after his day job. Now, fifteen years later, he owned his own restaurant in a good suburb.

Although Solan's restaurant was of good standard, his car was the worst Hillman Minx in London, and he realised the need to replace it. A search of car dealers close to, but not in, the same suburb resulted in Solan being offered a new car plus registration and road tax (I think it was called) with the Hillman Minx as a trade-in. The new car would be delivered to the restaurant, and the Hillman Minx would be driven away.

Alas! Solan, on the day of exchange, drove the wreck to his restaurant and then tried unsuccessfully to start it in order to drive his daughter to school. A taxicab took the daughter from the restaurant to her school. Solan and the immobile Hillman Minx awaited the arrival of the new car.

Two hours later, the exchange of cars took place, as arranged, but there was a complication in that the Hillman Minx had to be towed away by an employee of the dealer—an employee who was mystified as to why his employer would buy such a vehicle.

When Solan presented himself to the dealer, some weeks later, for the first service on the new car, he was greeted with a tirade of abuse from the dealer who had lost money on the deal—perhaps the only car dealer to ever do so.

Solan, unabashed, said, "You a Jew, me a Greek, there can be no winner, no loser. I will help your business. I will send you my relatives."

"No! No!" pleaded the man, whose self-esteem and bank account had both been damaged. "Please don't send me your relatives."

That story is merely to introduce you to Solan, whose imaginative dealings with the Chancellor of the Exchequer is what I really wish to relate.

It was mid-evening, and I was poring over a medical book when Solan knocked on my door saying, "Paul, feel like a coffee? The last customer has left, but I have to keep the restaurant open for another half hour."

What I was doing was rarely newsworthy, and so I usually listened as Solan expounded upon various parts of his life. On this occasion, he started to tell me about paying his tax. Believing that he was about to explain to me some clever method of cheating the taxman, I said, "Solan, if you are cheating the taxman, I don't want to know. Tell nobody—don't even tell your wife."

I thought that I had displayed great wisdom, but in fact, the wisdom was about to be revealed.

"Paul," he replied, "I pay too much tax, not too little."

He explained: "I don't want to be working here all my life. I want to sell the restaurant, in a few years' time, for a lot more than it is worth—and so each day, I inflate the number of customers who have eaten here. As a result, I have to pay more tax than I should. But Paul, in a few years time I will meet an Englishman who will think, 'Wow. What a lot of customers this fellow admits to having—but everyone knows that restaurant owners cheat the taxman. They do not disclose the real number of customers. And this one is also a Greek, so he must be twice as bad as the others. He must be making a lot more than he is telling the taxman.'

"Oh! Paul, I am going to be repaid all of my years of paying excessive tax and lots more as well, because an Englishman will pay me for a business with a lot fewer customers than he imagines."

That was fifty years ago, and Solan is probably today living on a Greek island in the Mediterranean. He is undoubtedly the wise and respected elder of the community, having made, I suspect, a fortune as a broker of London restaurants.

It is possible that he drinks coffee each morning with other old men at a wooden table on the waterfront, grapevines hanging from a trellis overhead, rows of bright blue dinghies bobbing at their moorings. He may well be receiving an English pension—why not? He worked hard and contributed considerably more tax to the English economy than was expected or required.

Just a Little Way Now

We must now travel thousands of kilometres to Karangarua Valley in the South Island of New Zealand in order to meet the other lateral thinker. Not only was it the Ides of March 1962, but it was also the commencement of "the Roar."

Red deer had been brought to New Zealand from England, Scotland, and Europe in the latter half of the nineteenth century. Similarly so, chamois were imported from the Austrian Alps and tahr from the Himalayas. All were freed into the forests in the hope that they would breed and subsequently be game for hunters, but their increase in numbers exceeded expectations, and by the middle of the twentieth century, they roamed the snow-capped mountains and forests in great numbers, causing erosion followed by silting of the rivers.

The New Zealand government's reaction to the problem was to station professional hunters in basic one-room huts throughout the forests; supplies were often dropped from planes. Each professional hunter had a "block" of land as his territory, and he systematically roamed it, shooting deer with an ex-army .303 rifle. After some weeks on a block, the professional would be taken to a new area and would undertake the reduction of animal numbers there.

It was estimated that, as a result of this culling, plus the few deer killed by recreational hunters, 100,000 were killed in 1960. Unfortunately, 100,000 were born during the same year, so the adverse effects upon the forests and rivers were unchanged. Successful culling was achieved decades later by shooting from helicopters. (France's forests are presently being harmed by overgrowth of unwanted vegetation resulting from increasing numbers of deer.)

The Roar is the worldwide name given to the mating season of red deer and describes the stag's roaring challenge to rival stags. The valley reverberates to the roar of a stag in possession of a harem and is soon answered by a would-be suitor who accepts the challenge of a fight, the harem being the prize. Not uncommonly, one of the roars will not have emanated from a deer at all, although sounding identical. It will have been made by a deerstalker attempting to lure an unwary suitor within the sights of his rifle.

It is mid-March when the Roar or Rut starts, and this is the time when amateur shooters abound in the mountains, seeking a mature stag with twelve or more tines on his antlers. Experienced hunters, professional or amateur, lure a challenging stag with an identical call that brings the stag rushing towards their rifle. Professional hunters living in the mountains and valleys were employed to reduce deer numbers, so they shot every deer that they saw—males and females of all ages—and, of course, venison was their main food.

Murray, who was not a big man, had thighs like tree trunks after a lifetime of climbing mountains on a daily basis, and the rest of his body was as tough as any tree. He had been promoted from the lonely life of a hunter to a senior job in a large town, with one of his duties being to transfer hunters between areas. The actual transfer would be by motor vehicle to the periphery of the new block, where the vehicle would be hidden before the two men set off on foot to the first hut on the new territory. Their packs carried weeks of supplies for the hunter, clothes for all weather, a sleeping bag, ammunition, and, slung over one shoulder, a rifle weighing nine pounds. Their heavy boots were studded with steel trichons and three-point hobnails to grip slippery rocks and fallen tree trunks. They wore shorts because long trousers, especially when wet, cling to the knees and make walking laborious.

The trail that Murray and the hunter followed would have been marked with a blaze upon a tree trunk every few hundred metres or so, but particularly at any fork in the track. The track would have been made by deer and was always in the open forest above and away from the dense, secondary undergrowth, as well as boulders and gorges that hugged the banks of streams and precluded walking near to them.

Deer would have chosen the path wisely, but nevertheless, there were sharp ascents, steep descents, mud, slippery rocks, glassy snow shoots, shingle slides, and an occasional creek or river to cross. There was always a grassy river flat at the end of a side-trail, and this was the deer's objective, their grazing ground—a picturesque green carpet surrounded by snow-capped mountains, bisected by a sparkling stream. Near one of these grassy river flats would be the hunter's one-room hut, concealed amongst the trees at the junction of forest and grassy flat.

There would have been snow on the mountaintops on each side of Murray and his deerstalker companions as they trudged the valley, and if it was raining, they would have been wearing either an oilskin parka or a blanket-like Swanndri—a thick, all-encompassing woollen garment that, even when saturated with rain and "weighing a ton," would trap the wearer's body heat and thus give warmth. Their knees were bare.

It was a hard life for hard men who loved what they were doing, were proud of their skills, and accepted solitude as part of the beauty of a life in the mountains and valleys.

Evan, who lived in Palmerston North, had been my friend for some years and had arranged for me to be allocated a block in the Karangarua Valley during the Roar of 1962. This meant that for three weeks, my party of four people would be able to wander the slopes and peaks of the Karangarua Valley seeking trophy heads without fear of being accidently shot by another group. The valley was ours.

We had finished the evening meal of venison stew and rice and were sitting around a fire amongst the flat stones of what is now known as Christmas Flat—the headwaters of the Karangarua River. Behind us was a small deerstalker's hut with its name STAGger INN scrawled in black paint upon its door. Three of us—Evan, my Australian friend Beresford, and I—had "staggered in" four or five days earlier after an exhausting march. My pack weighed eighty pounds on the airport scales and included a Paillard Bolex 16 mm movie camera, film, and adequate supplies of .300 Holland and Holland Magnum ammunition plus rifle. An untroubled Murray had joined us only the previous day.

"Murray," I asked, "can you tell us how you cope with the younger, fitter blokes that you take to a new hut for the first time? You are the boss, sitting at a desk all week, and they are as fit as young bulls. It would be human nature for a young bloke to clap on the pace so that the boss would ask for a slower speed. Does that happen?"

"Paul, you're right. Some, but not many, have a go at me, but they make the mistake of asking me how far it is to the hut—and, guessing their intention to walk fast for that distance, I always nominate a distance that is at least two miles shorter than the correct distance. All deerstalkers are experienced at judging distances in the mountains, as it is part of our job, and so they know exactly when we have reached where I said the hut should be, but they don't know that I have lied to them and that there are another two miles ahead of them. That extra two miles is a long, long way when you are carrying a heavy pack and a rifle up and down the side of a mountain.

"So, if it is seven miles and he thinks it is five, he gives me stick for five miles and then I watch as the arse falls out of him. They're all the same, trying to look around corners to see the hut, shaken when it isn't there. They never guess that I have brainwashed them and that there are two more tough miles ahead of them. Sometimes I even raise the pace a bit as well. The interesting point is that these blokes are fit and could easily walk twenty more miles if told that the distance was twenty miles, but they are beaten by their own brain when it can't understand what is happening."

Murray's story was forgotten as we spent further days hunting through forest and grassy slopes near the snowline—including being the first humans, for ten years, to find a way into the Troyte River valley. That was accomplished only because of Murray's bushcraft.

The day to commence our return to the West Coast arrived. Our destination on the first day was a hut in which we had spent many pleasant days during our three-stage entry to the headwaters of the Karangarua River. The incoming trip between the two huts, from west to east, had been arduous, and now we would undertake it in the opposite direction but with important differences between the two walks.

Firstly, our incoming group had consisted of Evan, Beresford, and me on a low track, unknown to us and not clearly blazed; but the reverse trip would be under the guidance of Murray on a higher, easier track.

Secondly, what we were carrying on our bodies was markedly heavier, as Beresford and I had each shot a Royal Red 12-point stag, a tahr, and a chamois — mine being a record at twenty-eight inches on the Douglas point score. All were trophies destined to be mounted, so the heads and capes had to be carried back to a taxidermist. They made for a lot of extra, awkward weight.

Evan carried his own gear plus my three capes (head skins) and my tahr head, whilst I carried all of my usual gear plus the large deer head and antlers slung over my shoulders and the chamois head swinging from my waist. Murray assisted Beresford. The weight of the food was minimal, as we had eaten most of it and were relying upon shooting a deer for the evening meal and subsequent days.

We set off with a spring in our step undeterred by the memory of the previous walk between the two huts. After about two or three hours of walking through a swamp and on tracks ascending the mountain range, we came to a kind of platform as the ground levelled out. We had a magnificent view back into the apex of the Karangarua Valley … when suddenly Evan stumbled towards the cliff edge, driven by the weight of his pack. We could only watch, as nobody was near enough to help. He immediately regained his footing and kept walking. Not a word was said.

Not very long after that event, we were walking upon a good track with good visibility ahead when Murray, who was leading, announced, "Two more short lifts and we will be at the hut."

I could not believe it. The walk in the opposite direction, nearly a week earlier, had been exhausting—but now, on a new route, we were as fresh as daisies and Murray had stated that we were nearly at our destination. How circumstances can change things.

We enjoyed the walk in the mountain air, the small birds showing no fear even to the extent of one attempting a landing upon my rifle barrel while we stood, resting, with our packs still on our backs. Our packs were, at that time, weightless, because we had found a suitable bank and backed up to it so that we stood with our packs and the deer heads actually resting on the top of the bank, with no weight upon our shoulders. We were resting in the standing position.

The track wound downwards, then after a short while climbed again, as expected, and soon we had crossed another ridge, then also the eagerly anticipated second one.

My spirits fell. There was no grassy flat as expected. Ahead was the same track, no hut.

I must have miscounted, was my thought as I trudged onwards a little less composed.

There was no misunderstanding when another ridge was crossed and the hut was again invisible. From a confident, fit, happy individual, I became an unhappy, tired, disillusioned shell carrying a very heavy load. Life was a drag with no apparent end in sight. Then the truth hit me: *Murray is brainwashing us. The hut is two hours away. Put your head down and keep right up his arse for the next two hours.*

My fatigue left me immediately, and I resumed my normal easy motion as Murray and I gradually pulled away from Evan and Beresford. Two hours later, Murray and I comfortably reached the hut at what is now known as Wounded Duck Flat and awaited the arrival of our companions.

We were hungry, so I picked up my rifle and moved silently through the trees towards the river and grassy flat. We ate venison stew and rice that night and twice daily until we reached our car two days later.

The Basics of Diagnosis

Half a century ago, I was one of a group of eight or so medical students being given an afternoon tutorial by a senior surgeon at Royal Prince Alfred Hospital in Sydney who stressed the necessity of comparison when diagnosing an abnormality.

"For example," he said, "when a patient complains of an abnormality in one knee, it is essential to thoroughly examine the good knee before seeking to identify the abnormality in the other one."

It is similarly so elsewhere. If a woman complains of having found a lump in one breast, it is essential to examine the normal breast first. You must know what her normal is before endeavouring to diagnose the abnormal.

He told us of an event twenty years previously. He had been working in a hospital clinic when a prim and proper female septuagenarian was his next patient. She, seated in a wheelchair before his desk, imperiously informed him that her left knee was painful. After some questioning, he arose from his chair and walked around the small desk whilst the nurse turned the chair away from the desk and lifted the lady's long skirt above her knees. Failing to inform the righteous lady that he intended to examine her healthy knee prior to the painful one, he knelt and grasped her painless knee in both hands, only to be rewarded by a stroke of her walking stick across his shoulders and a cry of, "You insolent young pup!"

Similarly, a woman might be surprised to have both breasts palpated when she had only complained of a lump in one, and even more surprised to have her feet palpated—which I would do to ensure that her arteries were healthy and normally delivering blood to her feet. If impalpable, I would have wondered about the state of her other arteries: those to her heart, eyes, kidneys, etc.

The physical examination of a patient is an art developed over hundreds of years. It is marvellous what conclusions can be made with certainty by listening, looking, feeling, smelling, perhaps tasting, and, all the while, by thinking, thinking, thinking.

All of my tutors have been masters of their art, but the man who taught me how to think through a problem and how to use the special senses, which we are all given, was Maurice Pappworth of London in 1963 and 1964. Hundreds, even thousands of other doctors would say the same thing: he was an inspiration. He taught me to love medicine and to practise and practise inspection, palpation, percussion, and auscultation.

It was impossible to win a debate with Maurice Pappworth. He destroyed my opinion many, many times, but always in a friendly and encouraging way. On one lovely spring Saturday afternoon, at the completion of a three-hour teaching session, he was driving four of us from a London hospital. The grounds were a sea of colour, and I commented that I wished I had my camera with me.

"You are a cameraman, are you, Moffitt?" he said.

I foolishly replied, "Yes, and don't challenge me on it, as I am good at it."

"What camera do you use, Moffitt?" asked my tutor.

Proudly, I replied, "A Paillard Bolex 16 mm movie camera."

That camera was what professional news cameramen were using worldwide in 1963, and there was no better handheld movie camera in the world, so I felt in control of the conversation until he replied, "I also have a Paillard Bolex 16 mm movie camera, Moffitt." Done again; it was impossible to beat him.

On another occasion, he put his arm on my shoulder and said, "I am particularly hard on you, Moffitt, but I think that you understand why." I didn't, but it was for my good.

Let me teach you palpation, percussion, and auscultation now. You will love them, and you may learn to recognise if your doctor is undertaking any or all of them expertly or inexpertly, as a useless routine, without any real expectation of producing accurate information. (Trust me, some even do it to me nowadays when I am a patient).

Palpation

Firstly, you need a small towel and a wooden toothpick, or perhaps a five-cent coin. Now, seated at a table, put the towel over the toothpick and place your right hand gently, palm down, on the towel just closer to you than the toothpick. Gently press upon the towel with the whole of your fingers by bending them at the junction with your hand (the metacarpal joints)—but it will be the pulps of your fingers that send the information to your brain about what lies beneath your fingers and the towel. You will feel the firmness of the tabletop; that's all.

Now, move your hand over to where you think the toothpick is and *gently* press with your fingers again. There is the toothpick. Now, double the towel and do it again. The toothpick is again easily found. Fold the towel into four, and you may not be able to feel the toothpick. Now press gently but harder, and you will again find the toothpick.

Of course, you have been doing palpation upon supermarket peaches and plums for years, so you might already be an expert.

Doctors are not trying to find hidden toothpicks but are seeking to identify the normality or abnormality of structures, the texture of tissues or arteries, reverberations of sound, the production of pain by gentle pressure or by suddenly releasing pressure, and many other things. The information is diverse and can be essential. X-rays, ultrasound, and MRI may be required for diagnosis in many cases, but occasionally only palpation can give the answer. Let me tell you of one such case seen by me after I returned to Australia following my years in London.

A teenage female patient from Belmont Hospital was admitted to a surgical ward at Royal Newcastle Hospital with a provisional diagnosis of perinephric abscess. This is a life-threatening disease caused by pus accumulating around one of the patient's kidneys, but it was complicated in this young lady by the fact that she was seven months pregnant. The provisional diagnosis had been made solely upon a spiking temperature, a painful back, and blood counts consistent with a severe infection somewhere in her body.

The surgeon had a big problem, as a perinephric abscess must be surgically drained, which requires a major operation through the patient's back, and he had no proof that the temperature and back pain were due to a perinephric abscess. Pregnancy precluded X-rays, and ultrasound was in the future. To undertake a major operation on this pregnant young woman and then find no abscess would be disastrous. So he requested that I should consult as to whether an abscess was present or not: a second opinion.

I arrived with my registrar Vince and a junior medical officer, in late morning. After the others, I palpated the non-tender loin before progressing to the painful side. Seated beside her bed, my right hand resting flat against her loin, I gently pressed the pulps of my fingers into her skin and then slowly exerted more pressure as I felt the deeper tissues, seeking I knew not what.

Shortly, I felt a crackling deep beneath my fingers. Adjacent areas gave the same result. It was like crushing eggshells under a blanket. I had never previously felt *crepitus*, which is a Latin word meaning "rattling, clashing, cracking," but it is so distinctive that I knew immediately that the young woman had air or gas in her tissues. As it could not be air, it could only be gas.

I said, "She has crepitus, so she must have a perinephric abscess due to a gas-forming organism." Nothing brilliant: just reading the unequivocal signs. My colleagues then palpated her back again and felt the crepitus.

The surgeon was delighted with my confident diagnosis, and the teenager was scheduled for immediate surgery.

"Are you going to the theatre?" asked Vince as we continued our round of patients.

"No," I replied.

"We don't have a clinic this afternoon, so we could easily postpone the other things, and that would then leave us free to watch the operation," said Vince.

So Vince won, and there we were at 1400 hours—wearing surgical caps, masks, and gowns—standing above the surgical team upon a long stool on the opposite side of the operating table from the surgeon, who was awaiting the anaesthetist's approval for surgery to commence.

My friend, the surgeon, raised his head and gave me a perfunctory nod before extending his gloved hand to receive the scalpel proffered by the nurse. Looking over his head and through the open windows of the operating theatre, I could see tanned bodies sunbaking on Newcastle

Beach whilst others were in the surf as the waves rolled ashore. All were unaware of the drama being played out above their heads.

Time passed slowly as the surgeon cut deeper and deeper into the young woman's back and his assistant used a sucker to remove the oozing blood. I was amazed at the depth of the incision, as it had been many years since I had last seen surgery upon a kidney. Then, unexpectedly, a squirt of blood shot from the depths of the incision to land on the surgeon's gown. His head shot up, and eyes fixed firmly on me, he shouted, "It is an aneurysm."

An aneurysm! If it were an aneurysm, the teenager would bleed to death within five or six minutes, as there was no surgery or surgeon available capable of repairing a perforated aneurysm—and an aneurysm of what and where and how, and with a huge uterus in the way. A quick Caesarean section would save the premature baby, but the mother would certainly die, and I would be blamed for her death because I had quite unequivocally stated that she had a perinephric abscess. I had even stated that the organism was gas-forming.

I had no friends in the operating theatre at that moment other than Vince.

Fortunately (for me and for the patient), whilst the surgeon was shouting at me, one of his fingers perforated the wall of the abscess, which I had predicted would be present, and pus flooded the operation site. Hatred of me was forgotten amid sighs of relief: it *was* a perinephric abscess, after all, not an aneurysm. The operation would save her life, and she would have a baby at the normal time. One minute later, I nudged Vince with my elbow and nodded to the exit, and we slipped quietly out.

Vince said, "I can see why you were not keen to go to the operation."

Amen. I didn't need that moment of horror as the surgeon yelled that the patient had an aneurysm.

Perhaps the surgeon would have operated without my finding of crepitus. Perhaps another physician, consulted in preference to me and not eliciting crepitus, may have suggested performing blood or urine cultures or some such investigation, which would have delayed diagnosis. Perhaps a delay may have been to the detriment of the patient or her unborn infant; I don't know. It is indisputable, however, that the simple act of palpation made the diagnosis and that no machine could have done so. Only palpation and the detection of crepitus had given the diagnosis.

It is an unfortunate truth that the crepitus was not detected by the teenager's general practitioner, the junior doctor, senior doctor, specialist surgeons at Belmont and Royal Newcastle Hospitals, my registrar, and my junior resident. A total of at least nine doctors had palpated that young woman's back and not detected the very distinct and crucially diagnostic crepitus. Somewhere, that teenager now tells people of the brilliant surgeon who saved her life when she had a kidney abscess during pregnancy, but she has no memory of the doctor who found the crepitus that led to the operation.

You can experience a similar sensation to the crepitus that I felt. Place a small ball of dry steel wool, about the size of a raisin or grape, on the table in front of you. Cover it with two or more layers of towel and gently palpate it. You will immediately feel crepitus. Admittedly, feeling and recognising the presence of gas or air in human flesh is a little bit more difficult, but try feeling the steel wool through a towel and you will understand why I was so confident that the teenager needed urgent surgery. I might add that crepitus caused by gas-forming organisms, such as in a perinephric abscess, is minute by comparison with the crepitus seen and felt when air from the lungs escapes into a person's chest/neck tissues as a result of trauma.

Percussion

One of the most rewarding manoeuvres undertaken by doctors is percussion. There seems to be no end to what we can learn by gently tapping on our patients' bodies. Would you like to learn how to undertake percussion? It is very rewarding, and you may use it to determine where to hang a picture on a wall, how much fluid there is in a tank, or whether it's a solid or cavity wall.

Seat yourself comfortably at a timber desk or table and place your left hand, palm down, on the surface in front of you. Now, fold the fingers and thumb of the right hand into the palm except for the "middle finger" or third digit, which you hold partially extended and bent so you can use it as a hammer. Being certain to hold the third finger of the left hand in firm contact with the surface of the table, strike the terminal joint of that finger twice, in quick succession, with the tip of the extended right third digit from a height of about seven centimetres. You will be rewarded with two resonant sounds. Now, move about five centimetres to the right or left and repeat the tapping, and keep doing so until the sound suddenly becomes dull. Look underneath for the cause. A partition? A post?

Why not now try it on a human? Use a bare-chested male or prepubescent female (breasts would obstruct what I intend to teach you) lying supine upon a bed or bench whilst you sit or stand facing the individual's right side. Now gently place your left middle finger flat against the skin and between two ribs about five centimetres below the middle of the right collarbone and hit it with your curved right middle finger, just as you did upon the table. Immediately, you will be rewarded with a resonant sound because there is only air-filled lung beneath your finger.

Now move your left middle finger down to the rib space below the one that you have just tested and do the percussion again—a resonant sound again. Keep moving down the rib spaces until the sound becomes dull. You have reached the liver, which is in the abdomen but protruding up under the ribs. Keep your left hand in the same spot and ask your friend to take and hold a deep breath. Then percuss again. Goodness me! The sound is again resonant, because the deep breath has expanded the lung, which is again beneath your left middle finger. The expanding lung has pushed the liver farther down into the abdomen.

I frequently practiced percussion with my hearing blocked by simultaneously wearing my stethoscope, as I believe that the sound produced by percussion is not only heard but also felt by the finger in contact with the chest wall: the left middle finger. The finding of dullness to percussion, when resonance should be present, is a warning sign to a doctor. So is the reverse. Have fun.

My most vivid memory of poor percussion involves another doctor and happened in 1964. We were candidates attempting specialist status in Edinburgh, and each of us knew that of the four hundred doctors attempting the examination, only about sixty would be considered to possess specialist skills and knowledge. The other three hundred and forty would fail. There would be four written examinations and five face-to-face examinations; we would be very thoroughly tested.

On this particular day, I was one of twelve candidates being assessed by a professor. By chance, I was the last to be examined and was able to hear the penultimate candidate's questioning as he stood beside his patient in the adjacent bed. He was known to me from time we had spent at Brompton Hospital, and I knew him to be intelligent and capable but also arrogant and super-confident. He gave a very polished and confident performance in diagnosing lung cancer, including a description of the man's fingertips, which were bulbous like clubs—a strange accompaniment to lung cancer.

My fellow candidate's performance at this stage was faultless, and I was inwardly cursing, as I had reasoned that my own chance of being successful on that day rested upon all of the other eleven candidates making a mistake while I made none. The professor asked about the percussion of the patient's chest, and Dr Arrogance stated that it was normal. The Scottish professor dialectically replied, "Oh really? Don't you think there is a little dullness here?" as he percussed an area of the patient's back over the right lung.

I knew immediately that the overconfident doctor—even though he had found important signs, such as clubbing of the fingers, and made the correct diagnosis—was going to be among the three hundred and forty unsuccessful doctors attempting the examination. Within ten minutes, it would be my turn.

Yes, my luck held — I was, but he was not, among the lucky sixty or so male and female doctors who did satisfy the examiners on each of the nine examinations of our skills and knowledge. You may be thinking that the professor was harsh in failing the doctor, as an X-ray would have shown where the cancer was, whether operable, etc.—but that is not the point. He lacked skill, and all patients should expect that their doctor is competent.

The examination is not merely a test of skills. The interrogation is intense, as repeated examiners search for a weakness in the candidate's knowledge, common sense, or competence. I had previously failed when I gave a stupid answer to an English physician's trap for Australian candidates.

"What is the cheapest way to give vitamin C to an English child?" he asked.

My brain was full of medical facts, and I even knew the sugar content

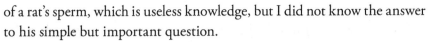

of a rat's sperm, which is useless knowledge, but I did not know the answer to his simple but important question.

"Oranges" was my thoughtless response.

"Does refrigerating an orange for months in storage destroy the vitamin C?" he asked—and of course, I did not know the answer to this either, which displayed even greater ignorance. I now know that freezing and heating destroy vitamin C and that the cheapest similarity to it is ascorbic acid tablets.

A month later, I did not bother to seek my name on the list of successful candidates.

My belief today, nearly fifty years later, is that I should learn something every day or the day is wasted. The source is immaterial. I might forget more than I learn, but to keep learning is the aim. The English examiner brought me down to earth with a great jolt, teaching me that knowledge is not attained solely from books. Life is a great tutor.

Auscultation

Another essential component of a physical examination is auscultation: listening to sounds produced by the body of a human or other species. We listen to the breath sounds to determine normalcy; the presence of added or missing turbulence in arteries/veins no matter where; the normal tinkle of the fluid moving through intestines—whatever the noise, we seek to identify it by use of a stethoscope.

But two hundred years ago, clinicians did not have stethoscopes. It was not until 1816 that René Laennec invented one—a hollow cylinder of wood. Prior to that, clinicians rested an ear against the patient's chest or abdomen.

Another useless piece of history is that a French army surgeon, Dominique Jean Larrey, is said to have undertaken two hundred amputations over a twenty-four-hour period during Napoleon's Russian campaign. Did the patients receive an anaesthetic during the amputation of the leg or arm? No. Just hold the man down, cut the flesh, and saw the bone.

As I said earlier, some procedural specialists do not waste a lot of effort upon clinical signs nowadays, as they know that their magic "whateverscope" will reveal all later. There are times, however, when the only source of diagnosis is the examiner's eyes, ears, hands, and brain—no whateverscope.

Let me tell you of one such occasion.

Anzac Day 2009 was special to me for a number of reasons. My troop carrier was one of six vehicles undertaking a 5,000-plus-kilometre trip through some of Australia's deserts, and we ten occupants had held a Dawn Service at GPS 22' 30'32"S 125' 15'57"E in the Gibson Desert, hundreds of kilometres from anywhere. Bob Burrage, ex-cop, our leader and the brains behind the trip, had planned the service with the aid of Dale Bailey, schoolteacher and grazier, both of whom gave speeches.

Bob spoke first and concluded with, "I was looking through a book of prose that I carry, and I came across this sonnet by Douglas Stewart. Its words still apply today." He then read the very moving sonnet that finishes:

> You see that fellow with the grin, one eye on the girls,
> The other on the pub, his uniform shabby already?
> Well, don't let him hear us, but he's the Unknown Soldier,
> They just let him out, they say that he lives forever.
> They put him away with flowers and flags and forget him,
> But he always comes when they want him. He does the fighting."

Bob then stepped aside on this red dust clearing, and Dale read verse 4 of "Australia Gives All" by Jim Kelly:

> Australia in all her young glory,
> Proudly she waves her flag,
> Scornful of peril and danger,
> Ties it to the highest crag.
> Remember the first awakening
> When brave sons answered the "call",
> They gave her worthwhile traditions,
> and remembering, Australia gives all!
> We all then recited:

Age shall not weary them
Nor the years condemn
At the going down of the sun
And in the morning
We shall remember them.
Lest we forget

I tried to speak but was too emotional. We then had a communal Anzac Day feast of bacon and eggs in that remote desert of stark beauty. These people did their service as loyal and proud Australians.

Our recognition of Australia's servicemen and breakfast completed, we entered our vehicles and drove for some hours to Jupiter Bore, which is situated in a grove of oak trees to the side of the road. I was eating a sandwich when a fellow driver ran up, yelling that another member had collapsed in his vehicle complaining of chest pain. As I hurried towards the vehicle, I hoped that the man was not suffering a heart attack, because survival by cardiopulmonary resuscitation in this desert, hundreds of kilometres from life-saving cardio-version, was impossible.

It was with great relief that I, accompanied by Bob, found the man to be conscious, seated in his vehicle, with his arms encircling his upper abdomen and lower chest. The pain passed off within minutes, and he was able to tell me about the pain and answer my questions before moving to his camp stretcher, which was lying upon the ground beside his vehicle.

Inspection, palpation, percussion, and auscultation were undertaken as I knelt in the dust by his side, with auscultation in this case being my ear placed onto his chest and abdomen. He had a large scar from recent upper abdominal surgery, and the possibility of adhesions and bowel obstruction requiring urgent surgery crossed my mind. But the normal tinkle of fluid in his intestines as I placed my ear upon his abdomen ruled that out.

I diagnosed simple intestinal colic and stated that he was in no immediate danger and did not require evacuation. A decision to evacuate him to hospital would have necessitated a six-hour drive to the Aboriginal settlement of Kintori, where there is an airstrip of sorts and where the Flying Doctor could pick him up and fly him to Alice Springs hospital. The whole exercise would inconvenience many people and be a huge expense.

It was a very tense time as the hours passed in the desert and I agonised over whether I was right or wrong in advising that everything would settle down. Then, at four in the afternoon, he suffered another attack. Again I found nothing upon physical examination, and in particular his bowel sounds were a normal quiet tinkle. Again I advised, "Wait and see."

After a pain-free night, a normal bowel movement, and breakfast, the patient resumed the driver's seat, and we continued our travels as though nothing had happened.

I do not know what action the group would have taken if I had not been present and making decisions, but all are calm, intelligent people, and I feel sure that they would have decided to sit tight. So I really was superfluous. But what if I had heard loud borborygmi indicating a bowel obstruction? The inspection, palpation, percussion, and auscultation were important for what they did *not* find rather than what they did find; they showed that the lower chest/abdominal pain was not caused by a heart attack or any other medical or surgical emergency requiring the Flying Doctor service at considerable expense plus inconvenience to many people.

Your Role Is Important

Why not put your ear against someone's abdomen and listen to the tinkle of normal borborygmi? You may as well then listen to that person's heart beating—the sounds made by the valves as blood is pumped to the lungs and body. Perhaps then put your ear against the left or right side of the person's chest and ask him or her to breathe deeply in and out. All of the sounds will be different.

A physical sign that all parents should be aware of and check for is the presence of a "stiff neck" in an acutely ill child or infant. Time after time, I see this warning given on television or in newsprint, informing parents that a stiff neck is often present in meningococcal meningitis (also polio, subarachnoid haemorrhage, and others), but no instruction is ever given of how the parent should test for this crucially important sign. Detecting it early may well save your child's life, and you must check for it whenever your child or infant is suddenly sick.

How? Raise the sick child or infant into a semi-sitting or sitting position in the bed, supported by pillows as and if necessary, and then do one of two things. If the patient is capable of doing it and cooperative, ask him or her to bend the head forward to touch the chest with the chin. If the child can do it, a stiff neck is not present.

Alternatively, secretly hold a small torch against the patient's abdomen and suddenly flash a beam of light toward the chin. The immediate reaction of an infant or child will be to bend the head forward to look at what is happening. A failure to do so suggests the presence of meningismus: a stiff neck.

If either of these tests is positive, your child needs urgent medical attention. Practise tonight on your healthy child and explain that you will ask your child to perform the same action when sick. Don't forget—this could save your child's life by assuring early treatment. Adults too.

There are many other tests that are used in special circumstances by physicians or surgeons, but they are not part of the usual physical examination that is made to find evidence of existing or future disease. This skill in the performance of a physical examination is not inherent in all doctors, and patients should ask themselves if their physical examination is being performed in a thorough and thoughtful manner.

An example of a patient's assessment of his physical examination is the following letter. Judge John Clapin came to me for a check-up and subsequently wrote the following:

> Judges Chambers District Court
> Newcastle 19/3/68

> Dr Paul Moffitt,
> Royal Newcastle Hospital,
> Newcastle.

> My Dear Paul,
> Never have I been more competently and efficiently examined medically, and moreover in such an atmosphere of reality. Thank you sincerely, etc.

> Sincerely,
> John Clapin

All people of average (or above) intelligence can make a reasonably accurate assessment of the competency and efficiency of their doctor's check-up. You might perhaps ask yourself, "Was my physical examination performed thoroughly or for show in a perfunctory manner?" or "Did the doctor check the arteries supplying blood to my feet?" or "Was it done in a hurry?" But your opinion may well be inaccurate for one of many reasons.

For example, a young, symptom-free athlete *might* require a less meticulous examination than the athlete's sedentary father would. Another exception could be if a doctor saw a forest of hairs growing on your toes, as this, indicating a good blood supply to the feet, might excuse a failure to palpate the arteries in your feet. So be careful in your assessment—but think about it, because your life or your quality of life could be the prize.

It is with sadness that I see the advent of machines replacing a skill with hands, eyes, ears, nose, and perhaps taste—but these skills are still the mainstay of diagnosis. However, we are fortunate to have had the marvellous advances in investigation, diagnosis, and treatment involving all manner of new instruments. Many practitioners still have all the skills in inspection, palpation, percussion, and auscultation, which I laud, while others not only have these skills but also possess a special skill with a whateverscope. Others require only their whateverscope to make a diagnosis and give treatment.

I would like to tell you now of a patient who was not permitted to give a good history, was not properly examined, was subjected to many expensive and useless technological examinations that failed to identify the cause of his symptoms, but then luckily was referred to an orthopaedic surgeon who happens to be the son of the marvellous obstetrician in the story "The Things We Do."

Having read the first edition of this book, he wrote to me, "Your obvious enjoyment and satisfaction in your work is shared by many of us, not least of all me, and it was a delight as a reader to share your pleasure in sound diagnosis based upon clinical findings, while at the same time mourn its diminishing emphasis with the rise and rise of technology."

He then related the story of a man who had been referred to him after many "imaging" studies had failed to elicit the cause of his complaint of difficulty in raising his arm. My friend, the surgeon, wrote to me: "All that was necessary, after actually listening to the history, was to ask him to [remove his shirt, face the wall, and] push on the wall." Just as the surgeon expected, one scapula (commonly referred to as the shoulder blade) was immediately moved backwards because the long thoracic nerve to the muscles holding it against the back of the man's chest had been damaged. The muscles, therefore, were unable to contract and hold the shoulder blade tightly against the man's back.

So with less than five minutes of good history-taking and a competent physical examination, my friend had made the correct diagnosis—a diagnosis (like the perinephric abscess causing crepitus in the pregnant teenager) totally impossible to make with technological investigations that waste a lot of time and money.

Technology and education are responsible for the advances in medicine, but the art of medicine is the essential base.

Making Ward Rounds

Hospitalised patients require regular re-assessment to determine their progress towards healing and this process is known as "doing rounds." Hopefully the result is favourable but often it brings surprises.

Imposters

A nice warm bed, an abundance of pillows, meals brought to your bed, a newspaper or magazine, your personal TV perhaps, clean toilets if you feel inclined to leave your bed, sleeping tablets if you ask for them. A first-class hotel? No! A public hospital. But it gets better. You can have an injection of pethidine or morphine every six hours if you wish.

What a heaven, and all free. So why not fake an excruciating pain and have a few days of heaven before staging a miraculous recovery and flying the coop? You might get away with it once, but not for long, and not upon a second occasion, as an alert flashes onto the computer screen and warns the hospital staff about you as soon as your name or alias or Medicare number is typed into it.

The present-day safeguards against malingerers were not always available, and I have had my share of fakers pull the wool over my eyes and luxuriate in a hospital bed while I tried to work out the cause of the mysterious illness.

In 1964, I had returned to Australia, and in January of the following year I joined the staff of Royal Newcastle Hospital as a general physician with the added responsibility for all patients with diabetes plus all medical patients in Maitland Hospital. My responsibilities could not be said to be minimal.

One of our defences against being deceived by malingerers during the 1960s was a tome entitled *Impositions Upon Public Hospitals*. A copy was available in every public hospital. The book gave an accurate physical description (sex, height, weight, race, scars, tattoos, deformities, abnormalities, aliases, etc.) of every known hospital impostor in NSW so that identification of the person under suspicion of faking an illness was easily made … but only if the doctor suspected cheating and had the brains to consult the book. Unfortunately, in at least one case, I stupidly did not suspect cheating, even though my junior resident doctor had made the correct assessment of the patient and diagnosed him as a pethidine addict. I was duped and failed to consult *Impositions Upon Public Hospitals* until after the impostor had flown the coop.

"A pethidine addict has been admitted under us," said my resident medical officer (first year out of university) at Royal Newcastle Hospital in 1965. Soon we were standing by the patient's bedside in company with the medical registrar (about three years' experience) and the ward sister. The ward was on the eastern side of the hospital, looking down onto the Pacific Ocean. A dozen or more empty coal ships were riding at anchor as they waited their turn to enter the harbour. There was no wind, the ocean was a smooth sheet of blue, the surf was a succession of rounded waves, and in one wave, a pod of dolphins was clearly visible.

The RMO recounted the patient's description of severe abdominal pain requiring pethidine for its alleviation and his own failure to elicit a cause for the pain or indeed any abnormality upon physical examination. The registrar may or may not have examined the patient at that time; I do not recall.

The sheets having been drawn down by the nurse and the patient's abdomen exposed, I was immediately struck by the presence of huge dilated veins like blue highways running from the groin to the ribs on both sides of the abdomen. Although I had never previously seen a case of inferior vena cava obstruction, I knew immediately that the patient had that condition.

The blood returning to our heart from our legs and lower abdomen is carried in a number of veins that combine to become a single large vein in, and on the back wall of, the abdomen. It is called the *inferior vena cava* (IVC). Leaving the abdomen, the IVC enters the chest to empty blood into the heart.

When the IVC becomes blocked (owing to a large blood clot inside it or external pressure from something adjacent to it in the abdomen), the blood in the leg and lower abdominal veins cannot use the IVC to return to the heart, and a remarkable thing happens. The veins on each side of the front of the abdomen enlarge markedly in diameter and join veins in the chest wall, and the direction of blood flow reverses. The result is that blood from the legs and lower abdomen no longer passes through the IVC but uses the dilated veins on the surface of the abdomen to reach the chest wall and then proceed from there to the heart: a long and tortuous but effective detour. Nature is clever.

The diagnosis was confirmed by demonstrating that the enlarged veins filled from below, not from above, and that therefore the direction of blood flow in the dilated veins was in the reverse direction to what nature had intended. Naturally, I prescribed pethidine—even though the junior doctor had made the diagnosis of pethidine addiction—and I commenced a series of investigations while arranging a consultation with a vascular surgeon.

The morning of the third day of blissful rest in white sheets with good food and pethidine—a Saturday—arrived, and the patient walked around the ward in hospital pyjamas and hospital dressing gown asking the other patients if they would like to bet upon the horse races that afternoon. He collected money from a number of patients and wrote their names and bets upon a piece of paper. Next, he requested and was granted permission from the ward sister to dress in his street clothes and walk two hundred metres to Newcastle station to meet his brother, who was arriving from Queensland. Dressed in his own clothes, he disappeared with his pockets full of the money he had taken from the other patients as bets on the races, as well as a presentation gold watch stolen from the elderly ex-BHP worker in the bed beside him.

The events of that day became known to me on the Monday.

"The IVC thrombosis flew the coop," said the junior doctor. Graciously, he did not add, "I told you he was an addict. You should have listened to me."

Belatedly, I consulted the book *Impositions Upon Public Hospitals*, and there was a perfect description of him. The IVC obstruction was long-term and painless, his weapon to obtain pethidine from gullible fools like me. My anger was great, my pride considerably damaged, and my inefficiency unforgivable.

My duties at Royal Newcastle Hospital included care of medical patients at Maitland Hospital, and a year later, my arrival was greeted by an excited RMO who said, "We have a case of inferior vena cava thrombosis in the ward."

The alarm bells went off in my head. Another one? An epidemic? *It must be the same fellow* was my thought.

"Really?" I said. "Where does he come from?"

"He is a prisoner in Maitland jail. He is in severe pain" was the reply.

The male medical ward was large, clean, and airy, with polished wood floors and twenty or more beds lining the walls. The ward sister's desk was in the left-hand corner adjacent to the entrance, and as was the custom, the most seriously ill patient—the one with IVC thrombosis—was in the bed closest to the sister's desk.

The sister rose to join the RMO and me as we commenced our round of the patients.

"This is Dr Moffitt, Mr XYZ. Mr XYZ has inferior vena cava thrombosis," said the RMO as he recounted the history given by the patient, then the physical findings and results of investigations.

I nodded to the patient but did not offer my hand, as common sense told me that this must be the impostor from Royal Newcastle Hospital, although I did not recognise his face. An intravenous line had been attached to his left leg and no doubt contained pethidine. I checked his abdomen to confirm the disease and to determine whether there were any palpable masses in his abdomen.

The patient had to be the same one as had hoodwinked me previously, but I could not be sure. It was time to bluff.

"The last time I saw you, you stole a gold watch from the patient in the bed beside you at Royal Newcastle Hospital," I said.

A denial would have placed me in a difficult position, but he did not know of my quandary.

"My sister in Sydney has it, doctor. He can have it back."

I turned to the sister, and pointing at the transfusion dripping into his vein, I said, "Get that drip out of his leg, and I want him back in jail within half an hour."

He had been receiving pethidine, a warm bed, and good food for some days before I sent him back to jail, so he was a winner again.

There is no doubt that I felt better for returning this thief and addict to jail, but the taxpayer supported him in either place: hospital or jail. Of course, there was also the unanswered question as to how he became a pethidine addict in the first place. Was it the inadvertent fault of the medical profession?

He had an IVC thrombosis that probably occurred during a previous hospitalisation, and it was quite possible or even likely that he had been given pethidine for too many days during the injury that caused the thrombosis of his IVC. Was his addiction, therefore, a direct result of a medical oversight? He was now a useless member of society, but had a doctor's carelessness with the administration of pethidine ruined his life? Should I feel sorry for him rather than dislike him? There are always two sides to a story.

Not all people who impose upon public hospitals are addicts. Some like the luxury, the sympathy, the company, and perhaps the freedom from a neighbour's blaring radio that a stay in hospital can provide.

Miss Mogey was short and fat with an apparently normal personality. A gynaecologist requested that I see her because she had an unexplained fever after some minor gynaecological procedure, and he could not send her home until the cause of the fever was diagnosed and treated. As is usual, I read her patient records fully and noted the sudden onset of large temperature readings interspersed with normal readings for some hours. Physical examination was normal except for an abnormal "murmur" in her heart. This, plus the temperature, suggested that the patient might have an infected clot upon a heart valve. Blood cultures would confirm or deny that disease.

The blood cultures were negative, and so another reason had to be found for the high temperatures. Then Dr Di Wheeler solved the problem. Di was a registrar who would later become a very respected specialist physician. She asked Miss Mogey to get out of bed and found a thermometer hidden under her pillow—a thermometer already registering a high fever. Miss Mogey had dipped it into her cup of tea, hidden it, and intended to surreptitiously substitute it for the one to later be put into her mouth by an unsuspecting nurse. Miss Mogey would then have the new thermometer hidden and ready for the next cup of tea, and it could have continued for much longer if Dr Wheeler had not made the diagnosis.

The heart murmur having been pronounced as insignificant by a cardiologist, Miss Mogey was sent home—then readmitted by her general practitioner the next week with a new set of symptoms. She was admitted under my care, and I quickly proved that she was faking disease and discharged her from hospital. Still, she had a short holiday in a warm bed with good food and pleasant company, me excluded. Out she went, and a sick person immediately filled the bed.

Belmont Hospital having recently been opened, I was relieved of visiting Maitland Hospital and given responsibility for all adult medical admissions to the new hospital situated about twenty kilometres away. A few weeks after discharging Miss Mogey for the second time from Royal Newcastle Hospital, I was about to commence my rounds of the medical admissions to Belmont Hospital when I was confronted by her GP. She was a conscientious GP and concerned that Miss Mogey was genuinely ill.

"Dr Moffitt, Miss Mogey and I are considerably displeased with your handling of her illness, and you may be aware that I have had her readmitted to this hospital. I trust that you can make a diagnosis on this occasion," she said.

"I was not aware that she had been admitted, but I assure you that I will be trying very hard to make the diagnosis" was my reply.

Leaving the general practitioner, I took the RMO to the female medical ward and said to the ward sister, "Sister, I believe that a Miss Mogey has been admitted to this ward."

"Yes, she has just arrived" was the reply.

"Well, she is a cheat and a dunce, and I want her observed by your staff every minute that she is in the ward. I don't know what she will get up to, but she will feign illness."

The RMO and I then left to see the patients in the male ward before returning to see the female patients, including Miss Mogey. Circumstances determined, however, that I did not see Miss Mogey during that short admission. I telephoned the general practitioner a half hour later.

"Doctor, I have a diagnosis on Miss Mogey. A nurse, on my instructions, watched as she went behind a screen, took a tourniquet and syringe from her handbag, and injected a black solution into her left arm. A vet had left the syringe at her home after treating her cat or dog. I don't know what the fluid is that she injected, but it was in a small bottle, and when challenged, she told the nurse that she got it out of her sink. I have transferred her to the Reception Centre for the mentally ill. It will probably not be as congenial as Belmont Hospital."

Miss Mogey was never again admitted to Belmont or Royal Newcastle Hospital medical wards. She was not mentally ill and was no fool, as evidenced by her false temperatures and self-administered intravenous injections as a means of having a very pleasant break from a monotonous life. The boost to her ego at being able to completely fool more intelligent people must have brought her great satisfaction.

Some impositions are only a nuisance, albeit distracting doctors and others from their real work and causing some expense. I have painful memories of one, as drunk as a monkey, his left leg in a steel calliper, snoring on a stretcher after claiming to have vomited blood. The casualty doctors assured me that they had spent considerable time questioning and examining the drunken individual and that they believed his story was fictitious and designed to get him a warm bed for the night plus breakfast. I tried to rouse the patient, who responded by swinging his calliper-clad left leg over his right leg in a vicious arc that ended on my poor shin. The commotion he made in the ward resulted in the police giving him a bed for the night.

Medical personnel have some tricks to awaken people who have lost contact with reality—for example, screaming teenagers who faint from sheer excitement at a pop concert and forget to wake up. The time of friends, relatives, ambulance officers, nurses, and doctors is wasted, and care of genuinely sick patients is delayed. One painful stimulus to return these people to consciousness is to grasp one or the other *tendo calcaneus* (Achilles tendon) and squeeze as hard as possible. Lean down now and find the thick tendon at the back of your own leg, just above your heel: that is your left or right Achilles tendon. Now squeeze it and you will understand why hysterically unconscious people suddenly come back to life.

Another manoeuvre causing pain without damage to the recipient is to press firmly on the nerve running through the *incisura supraorbitalis*. Place your index finger onto one of your eyebrows and run it backwards and forwards until you feel a definite depression or notch in the underlying bone. (Don't worry if you can't find it; some people don't have it). Now press hard and you will get a dull, sickening pain in your forehead above the eyebrow. That trick will also awaken the dreamers.

The Rolling Stones held a concert near Lewisham Hospital in London during 1964, and I happened to be the medical registrar on duty that night, which meant that I had to deal with any medical emergencies in the wards or casualty. All was calm and peaceful—no stabbings in that area—but suddenly, in mid-evening, the ambulances started to arrive with unconscious young women. The junior doctors handled it in the midst of seeing genuinely ill people, and I was only called when two of these young women could not be aroused by the usual methods.

Casualty consisted of many rooms, but the young women were in the general area, as were many other patients, all lying on beds and screened from each other's view by white curtains suspended on tracks attached to the ceiling, providing visual but not auditory privacy. The other two doctors were not fools, and they knew that they had already tried the tricks that I would use in an attempt to awaken the sleeping beauties. They watched impassively as I repeated the assaults on the Achilles tendons and *nervi supraorbitalis* with a conspicuous lack of success ... and then a rare brilliant thought came to my mind.

I dismissed the doctors and nurse, took my Ronson gas cigarette lighter from my pocket, turned the flame to about eight centimetres, and ran it up and down the sole of one foot of the first young woman. No burns, just plenty of heat. Ooh la la! She was up and walking out of the place within seconds, her shoes dangling from one hand and not a word said.

One down and one to go, I thought, as I entered the screened-off area in which lay the second Rolling Stones love-struck female. She didn't seem to like my Ronson lighter either and was soon heading off after muttering something that sounded like "runt," which was unfair, as I am short in stature but not a runt. Perhaps I had not heard her correctly.

The other doctors were already seeing other patients and did not ask me how I had awakened the recalcitrant pair. I don't expect to ever see a

Ronson cigarette lighter recommended in medical texts as a treatment for hysteria.

It is always comforting to have one's word corroborated. The opinion piece "Strewth" (*Australian*, 3 March 2011) quoted Keith Richards's memoir *Life* as he reflected on the mania of fans during a Rolling Stones tour of Britain in 1963:

> Usually it was harmless, for them, though not always for us. Amongst the many thousands a few did get hurt and a few died. Some chick [on the] third balcony up flung herself off and severely hurt the person she landed on underneath, and she herself broke her neck and died. Now and again, shit happened.

Well, that's life! Two of the Rolling Stones London fans, arriving apparently unconscious at Lewisham Hospital, received and responded to a genuinely warm welcome from an Australian doctor.

Psittacosis

If you do not know about *psittacosis*, you should. It is a disease caused by the organism *chlamydia psittaci* that is transmitted to humans from sick birds—commonly parrots, parakeets, budgerigars, pigeons, or a variety of domestic poultry. The sick bird's faeces contain the organisms, which therefore are present on the cage or shed floor and can become airborne in the dust, freely available for you and me to inhale. The infected bird commonly dies but may recover, whilst the human sufferer may have all degrees of illness, from a mild dry cough through pneumonia to death.

An epidemic occurred in France in 1892 and a pandemic in North America, South America, England, France, and Germany in 1930, with high mortality because antibiotic therapy was yet to be discovered. It is a serious disease, and care in handling birds, especially sick ones, is essential to avoiding this condition.

Belmont Hospital was opened with great fanfare in 1967 and was solely under the authority of Royal Newcastle Hospital for medical and surgical care. My role at Royal Newcastle, as a physician, was then extended to cover all non-surgical adult patients admitted to Belmont Hospital. This meant that, for a number of years prior to the appointment of another physician to share the patient load, all adult, male or female, private or public patients had me as their doctor if admitted to Belmont Hospital for a non-surgical reason. The permanent staff consisted of well-trained junior doctors who telephoned me daily concerning problem patients, new admissions, and similar matters.

Medical rounds are the same in most hospitals and consist of the specialist visiting each patient and confirming that all is correct in the patient's management, but the round is also very important for its teaching component. It is obligatory for the junior doctor to be present as well as the one directly above him, namely the senior or registrar. They are in training and, hopefully, learning from the specialist. The nurses accompany the doctors and are also learning from the bedside discussion. Other doctors or medical students may join the group in order to learn, remain up to date, or contribute to the discussion.

My medical rounds were routinely undertaken on Tuesday and Friday mornings, and it was upon one of these occasions that my group—which consisted of a very astute general practitioner, two resident doctors, and the ward sister—entered one of the few single-bed rooms available at Belmont Hospital. The junior doctor introduced me to the patient, who had private health insurance but no choice of physician, since I was the only one on staff. He was a university lecturer and was no doubt assessing me as I listened to, and questioned, the junior doctor who was relating the history of the illness, physical findings, results of the X-rays, blood tests, etc.

Basically, the story was that the patient, aged about thirty-five, had never had a sick day in his life. He had never previously had a cough, had no family history of respiratory disease, had not inhaled a peanut, had sustained no injury, had not recently travelled overseas, and now was febrile and coughing without sputum. An X-ray showed bilateral bronchopneumonia.

So the junior doctors had diagnosed, proven, and were treating bronchopneumonia, but knowing what disease the patient had was only half of the doctor's duty. Why the patient had it was equally important, and so I asked myself, *Why is this fit young man, with no apparent reason for developing bronchopneumonia, now suffering from it?* It was not a huge leap for me to suspect psittacosis in view of the absence of the above possible precipitants.

"When did your budgerigar die?" I asked.

"Two weeks ago," replied the lecturer.

There was deathly silence in the hospital room as the other doctors kicked themselves for not thinking, *Why has he got bronchopneumonia?*

I should have rested upon my laurels, but I attempted to gild the lily. Knowing that the budgerigar must have been sick, I asked how it died, expecting the reply to be, "It had the flu" or "It had diarrhoea."

His reply shattered me, and the room burst into laughter at my expense.

"The cat ate it," said the lecturer.

Not only was I robbed of my moment of glory, but the lecturer, who was sick and understandably concerned, was now also considerably unimpressed with the specialist who had been foisted upon him—a specialist who appeared to be more interested in his dead budgerigar than the fact that he had pneumonia.

Embarrassed, I tried again, as the laughter subsided. "Was it sick?"

"Of course it was, or the cat would never have caught it!" he replied in an angry voice.

My credibility was partially restored, but I was certainly not back upon the pedestal from which I had hurled myself. Antibody assays confirmed that the man had psittacosis, and the antibiotic, which the RMO had already routinely commenced for bronchopneumonia, was continued.

I forgot to ask the lecturer if his cat subsequently became sick or died, but I'll bet that one of the junior doctors, over the subsequent days of his recovery, had the brains to do so.

I don't know whether the lecturer still keeps budgerigars, but he has certainly been warned off sick birds. He knows to avoid bird faeces; keep cages clean; wear a mask and not create clouds of dust when cleaning cages; wash his hands after tending birds, their feeding bowls, and cages; and quarantine new birds before putting them into a cage with his other birds.

Psittacosis, or *chlamydia psittacci*, is common in Australian parrots and was almost certainly the cause of death in about eighty galahs that died on or near my farm in recent weeks. Each bird wasted away, becoming weaker each day until finally walking but unable to fly; their feathers were ruffled, and many had a greenish diarrhoea stain on their rear end. I feed dozens of wild birds and was concerned that the topknot pigeons might catch the disease. All others were probably immune. Naturally, I was very careful about disposing of the dead birds so that I did not catch the disease.

"Mummy will kiss it better," you may have heard said to a sick bird, or "Give Daddy a kiss" to an ambulating parrot as it deposits, on Daddy's shoulder, poop possibly positive for *chlamydia psittacci*. Please, never kiss a sick bird to make it better. Such an action could lead to its attendance at your funeral as a devoted mourner or perhaps as a silent companion in the casket.

Charcot's Foot

I must tell you about one of my patients whose nerves to his feet were destroyed by many years of poor diabetes control.

The shape of your foot depends upon the small bones being kept in their correct position by muscles holding them secure. Some pull gently in one direction and others in the opposite direction. Nerves to the muscles stimulate them to keep up a constant tension: agonists and antagonists. If the nerves are destroyed, as may occur in poorly managed diabetes, there is unequal tension in the muscles, with the result that the bones move out of place into what is called a Charcot's foot.

In a Charcot's foot, the bones of the arch collapse downward, and the sole of the foot becomes convex, with the person then walking on a lump in the middle of the sole. This soon produces a large ulcer that becomes infected. Fortunately, the pain fibres in the nerves are also destroyed, and the condition is therefore painless. This means the afflicted person can live with the condition and even continue working.

One such patient of mine was employed at my hospital, doing a useful job. On a number of occasions, when escorting a visiting physician on a ward round, I would ask the employee to stop work and take off his boot so that the visitor could see a case of Charcot's foot.

Then one day, when I had cause to visit a patient in a male surgical ward, I saw my patient sitting up in one of the beds.

"What are you doing here?" I asked.

"Doctor So and So cut my foot off," he replied.

"Why?" I asked.

"Dunno," he said.

A few nights later, the surgeon joined our group at the local pub, and I asked him why he had cut the man's foot off. He replied, "Jesus, mate, did you see it? It was the ugliest thing I have ever seen. I've never seen anything like it in my life before."

"Well!" I said. "If you will cut something off just because it is the ugliest thing you have ever seen and you have never seen anything like it before, I am bloody glad that my fly is zipped up."

I thought that the female doctor drinking with us would choke, as beer went into her lungs. The general commotion and ribald comments prevented me from asking the surgeon if there was another reason for the amputation.

The poor man had been employed and had enjoyed the company of his workmates and was then condemned to a pension and being housebound. Very sad—but you see, some people, including doctors, do not think things through. My father often said to me, "Sleep on it, son." He was advising against quick decisions, such as amputating a Charcot's foot. I know the surgeon fairly well and believe that there must have been a reason other than "the ugliest thing I have ever seen" for the amputation.

Contributing to Medicare:
The Pros and Cons

It seems to me that there are some essentials in healthcare, and the first of these is that no Australian should be denied healthcare because of impecuniosity. No Australian should die or suffer illness because of an inability to pay for healthcare; surely no one would disagree with that. Now, how do we give the optimum service with minimal taxpayer expense? One measure that has been mooted is an obligatory patient contribution for GP visits—the objective presumably being to deter unnecessary visits. My experience, albeit commencing sixty years ago, is interesting and may give some guidance but not a solution, just something to think about and include in the equation.

My introduction to general practice was in the coal-mining town of Cessnock in 1954 when I became the third member of a group, each with a consulting room in a different area of Cessnock. Our opposition comprised ten doctors at three different sites. I cannot recall how business people paid for my services, but 99 per cent of the patients were in the Federated Mineworkers' Fund or the Mechanics' Fund (these names may not be exactly correct) or were pensioners.

Pensioners signed a form that resulted in the government paying me ten shillings for a consultation in my rooms or twelve shillings if the consultation occurred in the patient's home. I do not recall any aged pensioner, in my eight years as a GP, abusing the system.

The method of payment by the miners' fund impressed me as soon as I saw it working. Each patient, or the patient's carer, would sign a form and pay my receptionist two shillings (twenty-four pence) on each consultation. The forms were sent, on a monthly basis, to the fund, which would send me sixteen shillings for each patient visit. The monthly payment by the fund was always accompanied by a long list of the patients whose consultations had been accepted and the information that a number of forms and names given were being held for checking. As a result, I was not paid for these eight or so patients. The reason for withholding a form was not given, and the refused forms were never returned for examination. It was always recorded that a small number of previously unpaid forms had been found to be correct and the present cheque included their payment. What could be fairer?

Being a slow learner, I did not realise, for a number of years, the significance of the constant discrepancy between consultations performed and those accepted by the medical fund. The light coming on, I penned a query to the fund and promptly forgot about it.

Months later, a few minutes before my secretary would depart for the day, she was telephoned by someone representing the fund and informing me that my letter would be discussed by the committee of the Miners' Federation upon the morrow at 9:00 a.m. in the boardroom at the Newcastle Workers Club. I was invited to attend.

My clinic would continue until at least seven o'clock that evening. A meal would follow, and then there would be visits to patients in their homes until ten o'clock or later. That would leave little time to prepare documentation for presentation to the committee at nine the next day. I went to bed thinking that I was not brave enough to confront, on the morrow, a group that would almost certainly comprise communists and/ or fellow travellers.

But it turned out that I was brave enough. It was a big room with a big conference table, and nine well-dressed gentlemen were seated with papers on the desk in front of them. Everyone was polite, and we were soon down to business. I was document-free.

The chairman asked the secretary, after I had voiced my concern, how much money was involved. That figure was completely unknown to me.

"Fifteen hundred pounds," stated the secretary.

This meant that the fund was withholding payment on 1,875 consultations that I had undertaken. At today's rates of approximately $36 per bulk-billed GP consultation, this is equivalent to the fund withholding $67,500 from me. Now, just for fun, multiply that figure by the number of doctors in the Hunter Valley: there were probably two or three hundred, but not all had coal miner patients.

Whether the doctors being short-changed were many or me alone, it was a lot of money and a convenient, even if inadvertent, means of combating an adverse imbalance between member contributions and member utilisation.

The chairman asked the secretary why I had not been paid, and all members of the committee were listening intently as we received the explanation. A two-centimetre pile of foolscap-sized forms, which had once been submitted by my receptionist, sat upon the table in front of the secretary. He lifted the top form and said, "This is a form submitted by Dr Moffitt for payment upon a consultation undertaken on a baby on 16 January 1960. The baby was not born until November 1960, so Dr Moffitt claims to have seen the baby ten months before it was born. Here is another form. It is for a consultation in Dr Moffitt's rooms with Christopher Oliver. Christopher Oliver could not have been in Dr Moffitt's rooms, as he was a patient in Cessnock Hospital on that day. These are examples of why Dr Moffitt has not been paid."

The chairman asked me to comment, and I replied, "Everyone in this room has, at some time in January, written the correct date of the day and month but, by habit, written the date of the preceding year. My secretary should have written the day of the consultation as 1961, not 1960; she was a year short. As for Chris Oliver, he is one of identical twins, and my secretary, seeing his identical twin approaching, has written the wrong Christian name on the claim form."

The chairman turned to the secretary and said only three words: "Pay Dr Moffitt."

The secretary of the other large fund was a patient of mine. He informed me one day that his fund was in danger of collapsing because of the large number of visits to GPs by members and dependents. He asked if I had any advice.

I told him that I was unaware of member abuse, but not uncommonly I would be asked by a mother to examine and treat two or three children with a mild "sniffle" or similar trivial complaint—all well enough to attend my surgery. The cost to her was insignificant at two shillings per child (six shillings for the three children), but the fund would pay me another forty-eight shillings, even though the only treatment required was a handkerchief. A pharmacist's advice on treatment could save the fund a lot of money.

My advice, which he instituted, was to insist upon members paying the doctor's fee in full and then seeking recompense from the fund. This was implemented and was immediately effective in reducing my patient consultations.

My eight years of GP practice must surely be relevant today. Some fund members or dependents rarely consulted me; some did occasionally; some with chronic illness presented regularly; and a small few attended unnecessarily. They were normal, healthy, working class people who paid a fee equal to 11 per cent of the total fee for each consultation as well as a membership fee, and yet both funds were unable to balance their books. The obvious conclusion must be that a normal healthy community used (and uses today?) its medical services more frequently than anticipated.

One fund's response to the gulf between membership contributions and use was to withhold payment on 1,875 consultations to me (the equivalent of $67,500 today). The other fund's approach was to force the patient to pay the doctor's account and then claim a reimbursement. Neither solution is acceptable for Medicare today, and the problem is more complex than in the past, but I am sure that the waiting time for a consultation with some GPs and the cost of Medicare would both be reduced if a patient contribution were introduced for those who can afford to pay. Unnecessary consultations will certainly be reduced, and Medicare will be under less pressure.

Arguments about diagnosis and treatment being delayed stretch the imagination, but repeated small contributions, such as for a child with asthma, can amount to a considerable sum over time and a limit must be set, after which consultations must be without patient contribution. Curtailing wilful abuse by some GPs and thoughtless overuse by some patients is necessary, but so too is a high standard of medical care; and conscientious doctors must be suitably rewarded. This, I am led to believe, is not happening at present—even though many are making life-saving decisions.

Clearly, the problem is multifactorial and difficult to solve fairly for all, but I do believe that a service, free to everyone, would be abused by many with resultant excessive costs and not give the high standard of medical care, which is what the majority of the medical profession would prefer.

The Doctor and the Law

It was 1972, and more than a score of empty colliers rode at anchor off Newcastle Harbour, the prevailing northerly wind forcing their bows to face north as they awaited their individual call to the coal loaders. The sun glistened on the sea, and I idly looked for dolphins in the breaking surf as I ate my breakfast at a small table in the kitchen of the fifth floor unit rented to me by my employer, Royal Newcastle Hospital.

Hundreds of sailors were manning those ships, but their well-being or even existence did not enter my head. Then a knock on the door dramatically changed my day—and perhaps the future of thousands of Australian seamen.

My friend Barry Neal was ushered in by my Swiss-born wife, Mireille. Barry was one of a number of solicitors and barristers I was likely to meet at the end of a working day in the Beach Hotel, situated midway between Royal Newcastle Hospital and the Newcastle Court House. Barry explained his early visit, telling me that he was in the middle of an important legal case headed for the High Court of Australia. His expert witness, a cardiologist, had changed his opinion, with the result that the case would definitely be lost if he gave evidence. Because of this, Barry was hoping that I would give an opinion in court in support of a seaman who was being given a raw deal.

While I finished breakfast and Barry drank coffee, he told me of the law of the sea as it operated at that time. Basically, a shipping company, on hiring a seaman, would guarantee that individual's total support in the event of an illness or accident occurring during the voyage—all medical expenses, including hospitalisation anywhere in the world; repatriation to his home; wages; and everything else until the very day the seaman signed on to a new ship.

There were two important exclusions, as I recall, and these were any sexually transmitted disease or any pre-existing condition. This would appear to be reasonable, as a shipping company should surely not be expected to pay medical expenses for a dose of the clap caught as a result of a knee-trembler in a back alley of Panama City. Nor should they pay for some pre-existing condition.

As an example, a mining company paid unnecessary compensation during my GP days in Cessnock when a tough coal miner from Bellbird Colliery who broke his ankle playing football on a Sunday suffered the pain until he reached the coal mine and feigned an accident on the following day. There was a huge financial difference between receiving and not receiving "compo." I must tell you that I was not a party to this deception and was only told of it. To complete his story (please forgive the diversion), he used his hunting knife to remove the plaster when, some weeks later, he and his beagles were hunting on a mountain and it was hampering him. Tough boys, those miners.

Naturally, each shipping company insured its sailors against illness and accident, and the premiums paid must have been horrendous, with the case that I was being asked to become involved in being an attempt to create a precedent, lessening the shipping company's financial responsibility. That was what I understood.

Barry told me that BHP had refused the claim of a seaman named Wanless who had suffered a myocardial infarction on board one of its ships. BHP claimed that his heart attack was part of a continuing disease of the arteries—a disease that had been present when Wanless walked onto the ship. In other words, they claimed that he would not have had a heart attack if his coronary arteries, which bring blood to the heart muscle, had been normal and free of disease. Of course, that was absolutely true, and BHP had a very strong argument.

But the ramifications were immense if they won the case. For example, should a sailor develop German measles whilst on board a ship at sea, it could be claimed that the incubation period of German measles was twenty-one days, so he had it when he walked onto the ship. A sailor developing a diabetic coma could correctly be said to have had unrecognised but existing diabetes for some weeks prior to the coma occurring. There would be no end to it, and Australia's merchant seamen would be seriously disadvantaged.

Barry asked if I would be prepared to go to court and argue that the heart attack was a separate incident. I told Barry that I would go to court on his behalf, but I also told him that I had no idea of what I would or could say to help his case. Three hours later, I was standing in the witness box with a Bible in my hand, and gentlemen wearing wigs were shuffling papers.

So the Seamen's Union would have the assistance of a diabetes specialist rather than a cardiologist in its battle for justice, but it was not as simple as that, because many legal and medical minds had spent months considering the factors involved. Questions would have been well prepared, opinions given, and explanations sought and disputed. The judge or magistrate would give his opinion knowing that five judges of the High Court of Australia would carefully assess his judgement.

Whose argument would better influence the High Court: the cardiologist's or mine? Poor Barry; he knew that heart disease was not my specialty and that I had been given no time to think about the case and prepare some arguments, and no time to do research. But I was all he had. Poor seamen also: I was all they had.

It is said in Two Up, our national gambling game involving coins thrown into the air, "That is how the pennies fall." It appeared that the pennies had fallen badly for Barry and Australian merchant seamen.

My opinion was given in two sessions because of an intermission for lunch, and I recall a legal eagle telling me, at the end of the day, that a statement made by me, in my pre-lunch appearance, had been widely discussed during the meal. After admitting that Wanless would not have had a heart attack unless he already had disease of his coronary arteries, I had continued: "Probably everyone in this courtroom has some degree of coronary artery disease, but it does not necessarily mean that we will all suffer myocardial infarctions."

Apparently, my words had made some of the solicitors and barristers feel that the Grim Reaper was lightly caressing their cheeks, and they immediately lost their appetite for takeaway food. I was just trying to help Wanless, not frighten legal eagles.

Months passed, and Barry never mentioned the Wanless case. Then the solicitor who had represented BHP, Paul Anicich, who was (and is) also my friend, said, "Paul, it has always been my ambition to one day feature in Australian law books, but you have beaten me to it, because the five High Court judges quoted your statement about diseased coronary arteries as their reason for finding in favour of Wanless in BHP v Wanless. I thought that you might value a copy of the High Court's judgement by five judges, and so here it is."

He handed me the document *Broken Hill Propriety Limited v Wanless* in Sydney on 24 November 1972. How thoughtful can people be? It was a lovely gesture on his part and indicates his character.

You may be wondering if this is the same Paul Anicich for whom most Australians prayed as his life and that of his wife, Peni, hung in the balance after terrorists blew them up in Bali during October 2005, killing and maiming many others. Yes, *that* Paul Anicich. Furthermore, he and Peni are alive today, and he is devoting time and his legal brain to the cause of other Australians harmed by terrorists.

As for Australian seamen sailing the high seas today, their medical care is protected because of the words, "Probably everyone in this courtroom has some degree of coronary artery disease, but it does not necessarily mean that we will all suffer myocardial infarctions."

My admiration for ocean-going seamen in general does not necessarily extend to their union. However, when John Brennan was their leader in Newcastle, ships' crews regularly donated much-needed funds to my Diabetes Education and Stabilisation Centre.

No Laughing Matter

The corridor was long, the floor was spotless marble, and there were no steps or stairs. The operating theatres were to the right, anaesthetic bays to the left. Doctors and nurses in white gowns, white or blue caps, surgical masks hanging loosely beneath the chin, mingled with "trolley boys"—men of all ages expertly manoeuvring patients on trolleys through the activity. There was no noise unless the chief anaesthetist, a large-framed tyrant, shouted at an unfortunate junior doctor perceived to be performing a misdemeanour.

As a first-year resident medical officer at Royal Prince Alfred Hospital, I had been allotted to renal surgery and was impatiently waiting in one of the operating theatres for the arrival of the renal surgeon. I had scrubbed and gowned, was wearing sterile operating gloves, and stood with my back to the operating theatre wall. My arms were bent at the elbows so that my hands were raised and separated at about nipple height — safe from any contamination. The theatre sister, who should have been a film star, such was her beauty, stood beside me, similarly gowned and gloved. Two "dirty nurses," so named because they were not wearing sterile gowns or gloves and were present to handle unsterile surfaces, such as equipment, blankets, and such, stood against the opposite wall.

The patient, a man in his sixties scheduled to have an instrument passed through his penis in order to view his prostate gland and the interior of his bladder, was sound asleep upon the operating table, premedicating drugs having achieved a superb result. A blanket covered his lower body and legs.

My role was nil. I was totally supernumerary, with "teaching" being the reason for my presence. Hopefully, I would learn something. I would stand uselessly watching as the surgeon peered through the cystoscope, rarely offering me a glimpse.

Following a nod from the beautiful sister, a "dirty nurse" moved to the operating table, grasped the blanket, and pulled it away in order to expose the sleeping patient's penis for cystoscopy. Never before nor since have I seen a penis of such magnificence; it was as big as a baby's arm with a mandarin clutched in the hand, or perhaps a fat trout, gasping as it lay on a riverbank.

The "dirty nurse," having returned to stand with her back to the wall, whispered and quietly giggled with her companion whilst the goddess stared at the ceiling and I, the floor.

Will the surgeon never come? I thought, as the minutes seemed to be an eternity. Suddenly a trolley boy, whom we all knew well, walked rapidly through the operating theatre door. He was fifty or so years old, of average height, with a distinct forward bowing of his shoulders. He slithered to a halt, stared, shook his head in disbelief, and said, "Jesus, Doc. You watch it, and I'll get a stick."

We were no longer pretending blindness, and the theatre filled with laughter. Fortunately, the chief anaesthetist did not hear us.

The trolley boy disappeared and did not return. The surgeon arrived, and the trout was subjected to a one-eyed, inquisitive worm exploring its throat and beyond.

But what use is a penis if it is content to spend its time asleep, permanently hanging like a piece of old rope, never standing erect and demanding attention? Impotence is not something to be joked about, but some of the sufferers, without intending humour, have made me laugh. I will share just two of their stories with you. Both relate to many years later when I was a physician specialising in diabetes and working at Royal Newcastle Hospital.

Impotence due to a glandular deficiency has always been fairly easy to diagnose and treat. But that still left a lot of frustrated men, including many diabetics who'd had poor management of their diabetes. The disease had led to damage of the nerves to their legs and, more importantly in their view, the nerves to the penis. The result was, and is, that the diseased nerves no longer stimulated the distension of the penis to produce an erection.

The mental desire to make love may have been intense, but the penis had become totally uncooperative.

The first real help for these poor men came in the 1980s when intra-penile self-injection of papaverine or prostaglandin became available. Marvellous—inject papaverine into Percy, smoke a cigarette, and a rejuvenated Percy would rise from his somnolence to begin the universally loved game of "hide the sausage."

A lot of patient education was required before a person could be given the drug and equipment to inject his own penis, and I decided that there was more in life for me than teaching men how to stick needles into their penises. Therefore, I referred all such patients to a doctor who was prepared to undertake the task. One such patient was Doug.

Doug was in his mid-thirties and had had poorly controlled insulin-dependent diabetes for two decades. His severe diabetic eye disease had been controlled with blindness-averting laser treatment, but his impotence was a constant source of complaint, and so I referred him to an expert on intra-penile injections.

When I next saw Doug three months later, he said, "Thanks for sending me to that bloke who looked at me prick and then jabbed a bloody great needle into it, pumped it full of somethink, and then walked out. I was lying in the dark with me prick throbbing like a boil, and then a 'dog' started to come. The dog got bigger and bigger, and finally the doctor came back in, had a look at the dog, and said I could go home.

"Going home in the train, I was sitting opposite a woman and her teenage daughter who couldna take her eyes off the bulge in me pants.

"I had the dog for two days, and it wouldn't go away. My wife thought it was the funniest thing she had ever seen and couldn't stop laughing. I couldn't leave the house, and when I wanted to move around, I had to tuck the dog under me arm. It's a bloody wonder me prick didn't fall off. I won't be going back to that bloke, and you wouldn't be laughing if it was yer prick what got jabbed."

Thank goodness I had decided against being involved in intra-penile injections.

The majority of my patients—regardless of their age—came, in time, to consider me as a friend. Consequently, we knew a lot about each other's lives. One such diabetic patient/friend was in my consulting room on a day in July nearly thirty years after that memorable day in the operating theatre at Royal Prince Alfred Hospital.

"What are you going to grow on your farm in addition to lucerne, this year?" he asked.

"Watermelons," I replied.

"You would not know a thing about growing watermelons, so I'll get two of my mates to do the planting," was his reply. The fact that they all lived about ninety kilometres from my farm and that he had not asked his friends if they were willing to help me did not bother him. He knew that, if he asked them to help, they would do so. I had purchased the unfenced twenty-five-acre river flat farm with ramshackle house and barn for a song in 1972 from a true farmer tired of floods destroying his lucerne [alfalfa] crop. Weekend golf ceased for me and farming began.

It was winter, and I spent many weekends ploughing, ripping, rotary hoeing, rolling, and hoeing again—about five or six acres, as instructed by one of the farmer friends of my patient. Spring came, and my expert helpers arrived to plant the watermelons. They then declined to do so, as they said that my preparation was not of the standard they desired. I did not give an excuse, but the truth was that it had been perfect two weeks previously when they were expected to arrive but had not done so. They departed stating that they would return a fortnight hence, and I remounted my tractor.

A fortnight later, the six acres were as smooth as a billiard table, soft and friable and accepted by their critical eyes. Planting commenced.

These farmers, who had had no real education other than farming, dug hundreds of shallow trenches, approximately 70 by 40 by 15 centimetres, in geometric lines. Two handfuls of superphosphate were then thrown into each trench, the earth returned, and a circular mound formed from adjacent earth. Finally, my six acres had been transformed into hundreds of mounds with flattened tops, and deep beneath each mound laid superphosphate. Their next task was to plant four watermelon seeds in each mound. A month later, the two smallest of the four plants would be pulled out and thrown away.

It was a perfect spring day with a cloudless blue sky and no wind—perfect, that is, for everyone except these men who were slaving in the hot sun with hoes and shovels. With their only shade coming from large straw hats, perspiration poured off them. We welcomed the shade of the barn at lunchtime.

All the local barns had been built in about 1912, and all were identical. The new landowners of that time aimed to produce a saleable crop and simultaneously use a small portion of land to supply some fruit and vegetables for themselves and their horses, cows, pigs, poultry, dogs, and cats. Their chosen saleable crop was millet, which was used in the manufacture of brooms at a nearby broom factory. My barn, and all others, was open to the north. We sat in the shade of the barn upon bales of lucerne, eating sandwiches and oranges and drinking tea.

Suddenly my patient, his straw hat resting upon an adjacent lucerne bale, said in a loud voice, "You have got to help me. I was trying to give my girlfriend a fuck last week, and my prick was as soft as aeroplane jelly. There I was rasping away with the sweat pouring off me when she said, 'Would it be better if I got on top?'

"'Get on top? Get on top? How is the bloody thing going to run uphill if it can't run downhill?' I said."

His two comrades, who knew the woman, were embarrassed and stared at the bare earth of my barn floor.

Thankfully, Viagra (released in Australia in 1998) came to my patient and his girlfriend's rescue soon after I harvested twelve tons (not tonnes) of lovely watermelons in February. My financial reward was poor, as the good price is in December and January when only melons from Queensland are available. The public had eaten its fill of watermelons during the Christmas school holidays, long before mine ripened.

What Happened, Doc?

"Is there a doctor aboard?" You might have heard this when sitting strapped in your seat at 35,000 feet: an announcement by a member of the cabin crew.

When I hear that request, I keep quiet, sit tight, and let some glamour-seeking quack sort out why someone feels faint. I don't jump to my feet shouting, "I'm a doctor. I'm a doctor. Please let me help." No fear. Not me. I keep my nose in my book. But an announcement like "Doctor required urgently at seat 51 in rear cabin" would have me and like-minded doctors rushing to assist.

The field of golfers at Merewether Golf Club on Saturday, 12 February 1972, had been expected to be as high as two hundred, and so the players were commencing their eighteen holes at either the first or ninth tee and finishing at either the eighteenth or eighth green. It was a Stapleford Competition, which meant that points were allotted for the player's performance upon each hole and added together after the completion of the eighteen holes: less competent players, such as me, like this competition because it is still possible to have a good score even when one of the eighteen holes turns out to be a disaster.

February is a hot month in Australia, and having completed my eighteen holes at about four forty-five, I was thankfully having my first mouthful of "black" beer unaware of a drama unfolding within fifty metres of me. Reg Deards and his good friend, Barry Leis, with two others were completing their eighteen holes and were in the process of having their final putts. Having commenced on the ninth tee, they were putting on the eighth green. Barry was putting while Reg held the flagpole above the hole. The other two players waited their turns. Barry lined up, struck the ball, and watched as it moved closer to the hole when Reg suddenly grunted, dropped the flag, and fell backwards onto the turf.

Barry realised immediately what had happened and ran to Reg, removed his denture and pocketed it, commenced cardiac massage, and asked another golfer to find Dr Moffitt in the clubhouse. (By chance, he knew that I was ahead of his team in the start-time and that I should already be in the clubhouse.)

Barry told me, thirty-eight years later, that as he pumped Reg's chest, he could see the messenger running up the steps to find me. So, thanks to Barry Leis, Reg was receiving cardiac massage within thirty seconds of dropping dead.

Millions of electrical stimuli originating in a very special node called the *sinoatrial node* in the heart wall cause the individual heart muscle fibres to contract simultaneously so that the heart pumps blood around the body. These contractions occur at a rate of about seventy-two per minute, and the process is known as *sinus rhythm*. A heart attack overrules the sinoatrial node and a newly formed, rogue centre dispatches electrical impulses to the muscle fibres in a very rapid, disorganised manner, which causes the heart muscle to quiver rather than contract. This is known as *ventricular fibrillation*.

The loss of the heart's pumping action results in a loss of blood flow, and the brain is deprived of oxygen. After three minutes, this results in irreversible changes: life is extinct. But the brain can return to normal if the oxygen supply is restored within less than three minutes (longer when drowning in ice water where the very low water temperature protects the brain from damage), and so theoretically a person can be brought back to life from death and have the same mental state as previously, provided that the blood supply to the brain has not been stagnant for longer than the crucial three minutes.

Cardiac massage is designed to keep the brain and other vital tissues supplied with blood during the loss of sinus rhythm prior to an electric shock to the heart jolting it back to sinus rhythm, with the restoration of contractions in place of the useless quivering. So Reg needed cardiopulmonary resuscitation until an electric shock could restore his heart to sinus rhythm.

"Reggie Deards has passed out on the eighth," I was told.

Expecting a false alarm, I left my beer upon the bar and walked casually behind him onto the veranda overlooking the eighth green that is reached after climbing a short, steep fairway. What I saw spurred me into a run down the steps and onto the green to take over the resuscitation. Having checked Reg's mouth and confirmed the absence of a pulse and heartbeat, I undertook cardiac massage.

Some people recommend a hard thump over the heart as the first move in resuscitation, as this may cause the heart to revert to sinus rhythm, but I did not try it; you can imagine the onlookers' reaction if I had drawn my fist back and punched the dead man over the heart. Besides, it would have wasted time, and I was keen to get blood circulating. I commenced cardiac massage and, talking to his three accompanying players, said to one, "Please phone for an ambulance."

I asked another find my colleague, Dr Fowler. When I asked the third to breathe into the dead man's mouth, he said, "I could not do that," but nevertheless, he commenced it immediately. (Reg's denture was already in Barry's pocket.)

I was kneeling with my right knee between the dead man's legs. My left hand was placed on the middle and lower sections of his breastbone, while my right hand rested on the top of my left hand. I pressed rhythmically to compress Reg's chest about five or six centimetres at a frequency of roughly eighty times per minute (100 is the suggested rate). He was not overweight, which made the procedure simpler and surer.

My friend and colleague Dr John Fowler must have been in the clubhouse, because he was soon kneeling beside Reg's head and, after also checking the mouth, commenced mouth-to-mouth respiration in batches of three interspersed with my cardiac massage. Most of what John and I said to one another as we worked on Reg is forgotten, but I do recall John saying at one point, as we knelt on the grass, "Do you think that we are winning, Paul?"

"I think so, but we are certainly not going to stand up and walk away with two hundred people watching," I replied.

In fact, we knew that we were winning, because Reg's pupils were not dilated. I was so sure of it that, when the ambulance arrived, I insisted that the stretcher carrying Reg be lowered to the ground halfway to the ambulance so that John and I could give a short burst of cardiac and pulmonary resuscitation. I was probably being a bit overzealous.

Reg had been placed on the left-hand bunk in the ambulance as it stood beside the eighth green, and this meant that John sat on the right-hand bunk and leaned across the floor between the two bunks to undertake his mouth-to-mouth resuscitation during our six-kilometre trip to Royal Newcastle Hospital. I was again perched between the dead man's legs, which caused no problems until the ambulance driver took a left-hand turn, whereupon I would fall off Reg onto the floor of the ambulance. This happened twice, with my friend John blithely renewing the mouth-to-mouth resuscitation upon the presentation of an unexpected break in my cardiac massage.

The two doctors on duty in the emergency ward had been alerted by radio and presented themselves at the back door of the ambulance to receive Reg, but I refused to let him go until the doctors ran back into the ward and confirmed that everything was ready to administer cardio-version. Reg was soon in the ward and connected to the electrocardiograph, with the tracing showing ventricular fibrillation, as was expected. Reg was dead, but his pupils were not dilated, so his brain was oxygenated.

Bang! Reg twitched as the electric charge surged through him, but none of the doctors and nurses was looking at him. We were all looking up at the electrocardiograph screen and silently praying. The pattern suddenly changed to sinus rhythm. The sinoatrial node had taken over. Reg was alive.

I cannot remember what was said, and I don't remember how many minutes or seconds it was before Reg lifted an arm and wiped it across his forehead, saying, "What happened?"

We were later to learn that he had scored so many points on the seventeen completed golf holes that he was awarded second prize for the competition, even though he was dead.

John Fowler and I were present when he received the trophy two or three months later to a tumultuous reception from the club members. The captain gave an excellent speech, which he ended with words that caused a howl of laughter from the audience: "The bad news, Reg, is that we have reduced your handicap by one stroke because we think that you were running dead that day."

John and I then gave demonstrations of CPR in the hope that we could stimulate others to undertake it if needed in the future. But no one could have foreseen the unbelievable truth.

Now, stories like this have been enacted thousands of times throughout the world and many thousands of people have died and had life restored in exactly the same manner as Reg Deards, so why should his story be special?

Because nearly five years later, on 27 November 1976, Reg Deards created, I suspect, a world record when he dropped dead for the second time on the very same eighth green of Merewether Golf Club, New South Wales, Australia. Barry Leis was not with him, and death was final.

Furthermore, Reg must have created another world record by (again) achieving second prize in a golf competition while dead. It is unlikely that anyone will ever take these records away from Reg Deards.

Finally, please learn CPR. Three minutes is a short time, so only you can keep that person's brain alive until more skilled help arrives. Please.

Ben, Vince, and a Thing Called Superfoetation

Vince was loudly barking the news of their return to the farmhouse long before Geoff pulled the ute into the barn. Ben, a young red kelpie, had an urgent matter on his mind as he jumped off the back and enthusiastically commenced a game of hide the sausage with an on-heat, four-legged visitor from Moree.

Geoffrey, farmer and cattle breeder, was boarding his daughter's bitch but had missed the fact that she was on heat. He laughed as poor Ben, having completed his first ever naughty, dismounted only to find that he was knotted—locked bum-to-bum because muscles in the visiting bitch's vagina had clamped onto his penis behind the muscular knot in its shaft. Geoff told me, many weeks later, that Ben had a silly, embarrassed look on his face as Geoff threw a bucket of cold water over the lovesick pair.

"She could be up the stick," said Geoff to his daughter as he returned the visitor, a fortnight later, to her cattle property near Moree. "Ben gave her one, but poor old Vince missed out."

Geoff's daughter was subsequently surprised when three of the new arrivals were black and white, just like border collie Vince, so I wrote the following birth certificate for the puppies with an explanation of their mode of arrival:

THIS IS TO CERTIFY THAT

Vince and Ben are both fathers to the Moree young lady's pups.

The name given to this process of different males siring offspring in the same litter is *superfecundation*, if all were conceived within the same ovulation. The number of pups depends upon the number of ova (eggs) released by the dog's ovaries. Theoretically she could have six or so pups with each having a different father.

When the dog, already pregnant, ovulates again and is again impregnated, the process is called *superfoetation*.

Of course, it is well to remember that the Moree young lady does not mind sharing it around. Hoping that this is of assistance, Paul

I did not tell them that superfecundation and superfoetation are well recognised in humans. An important difference between humans and dogs is that a human ovary usually gives off only one ovum at a time, and so there is only one baby. Should two ova be produced in the same cycle and fertilised by two sperm during one episode of sexual intercourse, fraternal (non-identical) twins result. If they are fertilised at different times, not necessarily by the same man, it is known as superfecundation, and fraternal twins again occur. The production of three or four ova results in fraternal triplets or quadruplets and, of course, quintuplets.

Identical twins arise from a single fertilized ovum which has divided to form two foetuses; quadruplets have been reported as developing from two ova in the same manner.

Normally, a pregnant woman does not ovulate, but should she do so, and should sexual intercourse occur, another foetus may join the original in the womb. This is *superfoetation*.

There have been many reported cases of twins being born, one black, one white. Obviously, the mothers had given off two eggs, and different men had fertilised them.

There was one very unusual case of dissimilar twins being born after in vitro artificial insemination, and the reason was shown to be faulty sterilisation of the laboratory's sampling instrument, which resulted in the woman receiving sperm from two donors simultaneously.

A very touching story with a beautiful picture of five little girls appeared in Sydney's *Daily Telegraph* on 24 January 2015. It was of the five-year-old Perry quads, dressed for their first day at school, with their older sister Chelsey. The five happy faces melted every heart. But the interesting point is that of the quadruplets, two, so the story said, were identical twins.

That meant that their mother, Kerrie, had produced at least three ova, which had all been fertilised by different sperms, and she was, at that moment, destined to have triplets. Nature decided differently. One of the fertilised ova divided to form two babies instead of remaining as a single entity, with the result being that Kerrie gave birth to quadruplets instead of triplets. Jessica and Imogen were fraternal twins, while Bianca and Emma were identical twins.

Kerrie Perry typifies some of the unanswered questions about multiple pregnancies. Why did she produce at least three ova simultaneously, and why did one and only one ovum, having been fertilised, form two infants instead of one?

During the 1980s, I, upon request, took my team of diabetes educators to Kerala in India to give a series of lectures on diabetes, and I was struck by its natural beauty. Situated on the west coast near the southern tip, it has beautiful beaches, forests, tea plantations upon the sides of mountains, elephants and other wild animals roaming a national park, plus charming people and good food. But I am writing of multiple pregnancies, and it was the French news, broadcast daily on television in Australia, that informed me, during January 2015, that the world record for multiple pregnancies was currently held by the small village of Kodinhi in Kerala. Apparently, there are three hundred and fifty sets of twins amongst a population of only two thousand families. Twins are so common that clothing stores always stock two of any item. The village lacks a resident doctor, but the visiting one states that he has excluded medications from the possible causes, and the only common factor appears to be that the twins are usually the firstborn of young parents. So we have much to learn about pregnancy.

It is time to return to the young lady from Moree. Dogs have memories, so I'll bet that Vince is still laughing himself to sleep as he remembers how he beat young Ben to the prize because his nose detected the Moree visitor's pheromones a day before Ben realised that there was more to life than eating and pissing on posts. Vince's philosophy was simple: all things fell into one of three groups. He would fuck the first group, eat the second group, and pass on everything else.

Sweet dreams, Vince.

The Beginnings of Diabetes Education

When Belmont Hospital opened in March 1968, care of the patients became the responsibility of Royal Newcastle Hospital. I was chosen as the RNH physician to undertake the increased workload, but I was fortunately spared the trips to Maitland Hospital.

Having been a GP only six years previously, I was aware of the medical isolation of many GPs and was keen to bring them up to date. So, after asking many and varied specialists from multiple disciplines at RNH whether they were prepared to lecture to the GPs for one hour once or twice a year, I commenced, in 1968, lunchtime lectures on every Tuesday for Lake Macquarie general practitioners. There was a new speaker each Tuesday, and the subject was chosen to improve the knowledge and skill of general practitioners, not to advertise the skill of the speaker. Different pharmaceutical companies queued for the privilege of supplying sandwiches. Those lectures to general practitioners have now moved from the hospital grounds to Charlestown, an adjacent suburb, and after existing for forty-seven years, are the longest continuing postgraduate medical education in the Hunter Valley.

As for patient education, at that time there were no structured sessions of any kind on any disease in Australia, apart from an occasional guest speaker. Patients knew only what the GPs chose to tell them. There were no prenatal lectures, and no lectures on diet, exercise, or returning to work for patients who had suffered a heart attack. A ward sister with absolutely no training in diabetes would teach newly diagnosed diabetics how to test their urine for sugar and how to inject insulin. That was patient education before 1975. People died, had their legs amputated, and went blind largely because of simple ignorance about the disease.

This is the story of my role and my reasons for involvement in diabetes education and management in Australia, but I was not alone. Many doctors, nurses, dieticians, and others were striving to improve a very serious situation and achieved as much or more than I. It is not a pretty story, and some people will believe it to be exaggerated, but it is not so. I am indebted to the countless people whose support, advice, and participation made the changes possible. It is only a small part of the history of diabetes in Australia, but it is important in that it is dealing with diabetes "at the coalface," where people were living a life of misunderstanding and ill health.

The GPs did not see themselves as teachers. Teaching in the midst of a busy clinic was impossible. Specialists in private practice were few and catered to the affluent, not the masses. As a result of these things, patients knew only the very basics of what ailed them, and even that was often incorrect at best and dangerous at worst.

A slightly better source of treatment and information were public hospital outpatient clinics, which catered to the less affluent members of society. I was in charge of one such clinic at RNH. My staff, another physician, a senior doctor, two junior doctors, a senior nurse, a dietician, a podiatrist, and I treated large numbers of diabetic patients in clinics held twice weekly. There was no sense of urgency during a clinic, but time was limited and left minimal opportunity for education concerning diabetes. One patient would ask whether insulin should be taken on a day of illness with loss of appetite or vomiting, and another would have a different concern. I was worried, as I knew that each patient should be informed of both matters and many, many more, but we were giving only a small amount of information to each patient.

Undertaking a diabetes clinic was not for the faint-hearted. How would you feel if you had to counsel and advise an intelligent, worthwhile citizen, age thirty, blinded and with feet deformed by poorly treated diabetes? How would you feel knowing that it had been caused by poor medical management over twenty years? Such people were not rare, and they are still around today. I recall one such patient who came, like hundreds of others, under my care far too late to be helped stating to an audience, before dying prematurely of a heart attack, "I was born too early." He knew that his blindness and poor health resulted from twenty or so years of his and his doctor's poor understanding of the management of diabetes.

It was impossible to give our patients all the necessary information in the clinics, so the obvious solution was to hold group meetings where experts—such as our dietician, nurses, podiatrist, and my fellow physician Jack Fowler and I—could lecture a hundred people at once and answer questions from the audience.

When I explained the plan to the superintendent of RNH, he immediately granted the use of a hospital lecture theatre. Free lectures at the Diabetes Education Centre, the first in Australia, commenced on 4 September 1972 and continued for three hours in the morning and again in the evening of the first Monday of every month for three years thereafter.

The diabetic person's hunger for education and understanding of the disease was shown by the attendance of 143 people on the first day. There had been only one small article, in the *Newcastle Herald* and *Miners' Advocate* on 29 August, to advertise the coming lectures, but the attendees had come from as far afield as Sydney and Wollongong. There was no doubt that patients desired to learn about their disease.

Nothing is ever perfect, and it soon became apparent that there was a major deficiency in our lectures, and one of absolute importance. I had designed the lectures to be available to the public as well as our patients, but I had not anticipated that many people not associated with our clinic would ask questions about their own personal medical problems, which we were ethically forbidden to answer. It is customary, and rightly so, that a doctor does not criticise another doctor, and we were held to this when members of the audience would seek advice about their treatment—treatment that was often awfully wrong. We could not tell them the truth and had to be very diplomatic in answering. It was a serious weakness.

Those original lectures—directed at all diabetic patients, whether receiving insulin or not—continued for three years, during which time we prepared the new education and treatment courses. Diabetics belong to one of two distinct groups: those requiring insulin and those not requiring it. The former were the most urgent and were to be our first concern.

We knew that we had to plan a course at which all patients would have their GP's referral, including the understanding that we could change all existing treatment, as it is pointless to educate a patient who is receiving wrong treatment. Planning of the content and duration of the new course was straightforward, but the overall planning was not. We spent many hours in discussion until finally I was ready to approach the hospital administrators with my proposal. It was for a five-day outpatient education course, including the adjustment of insulin dosage and management of other diseases. The patients would return to their homes or alternative accommodation each evening.

Basically, I was requesting an area consisting of at least six consulting rooms, reception, laboratory, lecture theatre, and toilets. Facilities for sleeping would also have to be found for people who could not return, because of distance, to their own home overnight. I requested a full-time nurse, dietician, and secretary.

Such a centre would, I predicted, lower the existing burden of hospitalisations for diabetes at RNH by reducing short-term and long-term complications, but especially by nevermore admitting patients to hospital for the commencement of, or changing the dosage of, insulin. Giving a patient an injection of insulin for the first time, such as a newly diagnosed patient or an older patient being converted from tablets to insulin, and then sending the patient home overnight was unheard of in 1975, but I promised to do it. A newly diagnosed type 1 (insulin requiring) patient anywhere in Australia before 1975 was hospitalised for up to ten days, but I was planning no days in hospital. That would, I believed, create an immediate fall in hospital-bed occupancy by diabetic patients.

The superintendent, Dr Elwin Currow, and the director of medical services, Dr Jack Toohey, were men of vision, and I was granted, in mid-1975, all that I had requested.

Putting it on paper had been the easy part. Now I had to produce the first Diabetes Education and Stabilisation Centre in Australia. Five years previously, I had spent sixteen weeks at sixteen leading diabetes centres in the English-speaking world, and I had attended group lectures in Boston and Seattle. But nowhere had I seen an education and stabilisation course such as I envisaged. This did not mean, however, that such a course did not exist; and if it did, I should visit it and learn from their experience. So I set off on another trip, in economy class and short of pocket money, to revisit many of the centres plus three that Professor John Turtle from the University of Sydney and a recognised leader in the management of diabetes had informed me were doing similar things to what I proposed.

The new people I visited were Professor Zvi Laron, a paediatrician in Israel; Professor Leona Miller in Los Angeles; and Professor Donnel Etzwiler in Minneapolis. What lovely people they were, with the latter two subsequently visiting my new centre in Newcastle. Elsewhere, apart from Norway, little interest was shown in my plans, but Switzerland was, unbeknown to me, stirring.

As usual, I learnt a lot, but the important things were, firstly, that Donnel Etzwiler was already undertaking exactly the program that I had envisaged and so I did not need to change my plans; and secondly, that according to him it was labour-intensive and could only be undertaken on alternate weeks, so I had to abandon my original plan for weekly courses.

The investigatory trip at its end, I certainly knew, more than any other Australian, what was being undertaken on the world stage in educating people concerning the treatment of diabetes. I was a passenger on a plane from Sydney to Newcastle, and as I looked through the window, I could see, six hundred metres below me, white-crested waves curling around the base of the cliffs, the sea a brilliant blue with occasional flashes of sunlight reflected from the wind-driven surface waves. The plane was designed to carry only six or seven passengers, and all seats were occupied.

I closed my eyes, rested my head against the window, and dozed—until, about fifteen minutes later, a violent shaking of the small plane aroused me. Opening my eyes and expecting turbulence, I saw that the cause of the jerking was an irregular direction of flight. One minute we were flying straight ahead and the next turning left, soon returning to centre before repeating the cycle. To add to my concern, the left engine stopped.

There was complete silence except for the father of a young boy, who did not let his son know of our predicament. For the next twenty minutes, he quietly spoke to his son about various things. If we were to die, that boy would be spared any fear.

I was on the point of achieving a dream that I had been working towards for the past three years, and I was not prepared to die. I took off my coat and shoes and then refastened my seatbelt as I eyed a small fishing boat below.

The plane's gyrations ceased when the engine stopped, and the pilot turned the aircraft back towards Sydney. It took an eternity, as we seemed to crawl through the sky until, at last, we crossed Sydney Harbour, with the tall buildings appearing to wave long, beckoning fingers towards us. Then Mascot Airport was in sight, with three fire engines lining the runway as we landed. Soon the small door was pulled open, and we disembarked. I was the last to leave. A ground staff member, in a uniform befitting a rear admiral, said, "The toilets are the first door on the left after you enter, sir."

His concern was appreciated, but I could not resist saying, "It's too late, mate."

The rear admiral cast a hasty look at my trousers and stood well back. Within an hour, we were on another flight to Newcastle. One of us, a country boy, had had his first and last ride in an aeroplane and was boarding a train at Central Railway Station.

The Diabetes Education and Stabilisation Centre—the first of its kind in Australia—commenced in Newcastle on 1 September 1975. The number of patients per course was eight, but this number proved to be too few, because patients applied from all parts of Australia. After six months of operation, only nine vacancies remained for the following eight months of 1976.

Furthermore, these intra- and interstate patients were often suffering conditions (such as serious infections) that necessitated hospitalisation at RNH rather than merely attendance at the diabetes stabilisation course. The result of the influx of interstate patients with acute complications was, therefore, an increase in the number of hospital beds occupied by diabetic patients. And so, after the anticipated initial fall in hospital bed occupancy, the number of patients in hospital returned to the same as it was before the centre commenced, but the beds were not occupied by Newcastle patients—they were out-of-towners. A second nurse educator was appointed, and patient numbers at each course were then increased to twelve. There was an immediate and marked reduction in patients admitted to our hospital in spite of continuing referrals from up to four thousand kilometres away. Two-thirds of our patients came from New South Wales, but every third patient had travelled from other Australian states, New Zealand, and New Guinea.

Our plan was to train as many doctors and allied health professionals from Australia and elsewhere as possible, and 937 attended for four consecutive days or more of training. We did not record statistics regarding the multiple observers for shorter durations. They came from Australia, New Zealand, Fiji, and Samoa, which indicated the widespread desire of those professionals to be involved in the new concept of patient education. It was apparent that Australia and the Pacific were taking note of what was happening in Newcastle.

Statistics revealed that within eighteen months, there was a very large reduction of 1,400 days per year in hospital-bed occupancy by diabetic patients at RNH. These were the only statistics ever produced in Australia demonstrating a reduction in hospital-bed occupancy as a direct result of such a centre. Indeed, I was subsequently in the audience at a diabetes conference when a German professor, during his lecture, showed my graph (below) as an example of what could be achieved. He subsequently told me that he showed my graph to every group of his German students.

Running such a service to its fullest requires money. Apart from government grants, we depended upon community donations through the Lions Clubs of 201 N3, urged on by Rod Scot, timber merchant, donating $45,660 in June 1976. Many others also made donations.

Bed Occupancy due to Type 1 Diabetes

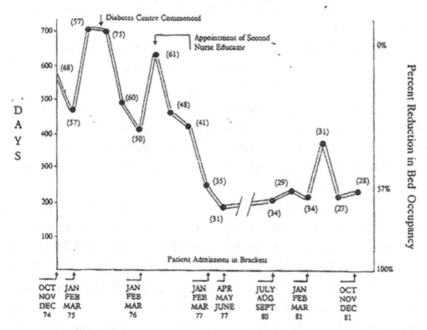

The problem of educating and treating insulin-requiring patients having been dealt with, it was time to confront other serious problems. The first was the very large group of patients who were managed on diet alone or diet and tablets and who commonly thought that they only had "a touch of sugar." Not generally recognised by doctors or patients at that time was the fact that poor control of this condition leads to blindness, gangrene, and all sorts of nasties—so they had to be educated about their condition and shown how to avoid the complications.

The second and more urgent problem to me was that there were eight thousand diabetics in the Hunter Valley. World research had shown that diabetes was the commonest cause of blindness in people under the age of sixty-five and that one in every ten diabetics in the mid-1970s would become blind. Articles in world medical journals indicated that blindness caused by diabetes could be prevented by using a laser to eradicate the diseased area at the back of the patient's eyes, but only a specially trained ophthalmologist could select those requiring treatment, and no such person existed in Newcastle. Nor was there an ophthalmologist experienced in using a laser—and of course, there was no laser. The problem of blindness was urgent. I thought long and hard, and the simple solution came to me after discussing it with ophthalmologist Dr Paul Beaumont: ask Fred Hollows for help.

So I wrote to and then went to see Professor Hollows. He asked me many questions, but he already knew of my centre and was receptive. He requested and received some assurances from me, and then he solved my problem. Basically, he promised to set up a unit in Newcastle to examine and treat, with or without laser, the eyes of all of my patients (and other diabetics), provided that I agreed to permit epidemiological research, which would answer a lot of the unknown questions concerning diabetic eye disease in Australia.

He sent me a young doctor, Paul Mitchell, whom he had trained but who was yet to become an ophthalmologist. Paul, with a great deal of guidance and involvement from ophthalmologist Paul Beaumont, commenced in Newcastle Australia's first Diabetes Eye Service. It was dedicated to diagnosing and treating eye disease in diabetic people and epidemiological research. He examined every one of my patients and hundreds of others. His thesis in 1981 answered many of the unknowns, and as expected, he found the patients with visually threatening retinopathy and treated them with laser to prevent blindness.

General practitioners and ophthalmologists were supportive, even though the latter suffered a temporary reduction in patient numbers because I and other doctors, including the other ophthalmologists, were referring our diabetic patients to the Diabetes Eye Service. However, one disgruntled ophthalmologist made a serious attempt to destroy my work. The achievements of the Diabetes Education and Stabilisation Centre were well known, and the board of directors of the RNH had sent written congratulations to me, so I was quite relaxed when asked to attend a board of directors meeting on a certain day. Expecting to be asked some routine questions, I entered the boardroom unaware that I was about to be attacked. I was shown to a chair near the head of a long table around which there were probably sixteen people seated, and after greetings, the chairman asked an ophthalmologist to address the meeting.

Until that moment, I had been unaware of his presence, but I was quickly attentive as he began, "I don't know how Dr Moffitt did it, but—" and then launched an attack upon my ethics in opening a private ophthalmological practice that was financially sustained through Medicare. Having spoken, he stood and prepared to leave the boardroom. I was shocked, but I knew that I could not let him make such charges and then leave, so I said, "You cannot make statements like that without hearing my reply, so stop there."

It took me only a few sentences to explain to the board of directors the need to prevent blindness and how I was doing it. My accuser was not heard from again. Many people were saved from blindness. Dr Mitchell became and remains world famous, and his statistics were important in an Australia-wide attack on diabetic retinopathy.

I had never liked that ophthalmologist to whom I never spoke, even though our paths had occasionally crossed in RNH. His complaint to the board of directors did not delay or divert efforts to combat blindness, and on 16 January 1991, Dr H. W. Thyer, president of the Royal Australian College of Ophthalmologists, wrote the following to me: "Professor Moffitt, the College is most grateful for the enormous effort you and the Diabetic Retinopathy Sub-committee have undertaken on behalf of the

Australian community in making everyone aware of the sight threatening complication of diabetes and the efficacy of laser treatment."

Paul Mitchell has been appointed a member of the Order of Australia and is a globally recognised professor, lecturing all over the world. Paul Beaumont has also been awarded membership of the Order of Australia for his work in macular degeneration. Having contributed so much to diabetes eye disease in Australia, he added macular degeneration to his field of expertise. Professor Hollows does not require further comment here, except to say that he was a great humanitarian, and his work lives on.

The next problem was to see to the education of and correct, if necessary, the treatment of the thousands of diabetic patients living in the Hunter Valley who did not require insulin. GPs could not be expected to be diabetes educators, so obviously I had to supply educators to cover the hundreds of square kilometres. The solution could only be to commence satellite diabetes centres in the communities where the patients lived—centres that would work in harmony with the local GP and keep him or her in the loop.

Simple. All I had to do was wave my magic wand to obtain space in community centres or smaller hospitals in the valley, pluck eight more staff out of the air, train them, and then convince 350 GPs to trust me to not steal their patients. Easy.

The first step was to prepare and send a proposal to the New South Wales Department of Health explaining the burden to our health services of patients with gangrene, amputations, heart attacks, blindness, and kidney failure, along with my proposed solution and request for eight staff to spread through the proposed satellite community centres. Concurrently, the Australian Diabetes Society (doctors and scientists) delegated me to approach the federal government requesting nine nurses or dieticians to be added to existing diabetes units in Australia's capital cities so that those units could undertake patient education and stabilisation as I had done in Newcastle. Stressing the benefits to the diabetic patient and the marked reduction in hospital-bed occupancy shown in Newcastle, I wrote to then Minister for Health Ralph Hunt and received an appointment to Parliament House, Canberra.

Ralph Hunt was overseas and I was greeted by a representative of the Department of Health and Dr Proust. We were still standing when the former opened the conversation with, "Dr Moffitt, we are not convinced that other doctors could do or would do what you have done in Newcastle, so the answer to your request for nine staff nationally is no."

Before I could speak, he continued, "However, we are granting you eight more staff for your new satellite centres for type 2 diabetes in the Hunter."

I was completely surprised, as I had applied to the NSW Department of Health and was unaware that they had passed the request on to the federal government.

So was born, on 18 September 1979, the Diabetes Education Service—the first service in Australia dedicated to the education of type 2 diabetics. It still exists today, although it has changed in character.

The service commenced at Royal Newcastle, Wallsend, Belmont, and Cessnock hospitals and in Maitland, with a mobile staff of five nurses, two dietitians, one secretary, and volunteer cooks. During the following six years, there were 2,391 patient referrals from GPs and 18,235 consultations undertaken. Again, it was apparent that Australian patients wanted to be involved in the management of their disease and that GPs welcomed the expert assistance of nurses, dietitians, and podiatrists in managing their patients' ailments. Much more was needed, however. How could I educate the GPs about the correct drugs to use and how to use them?

I composed a flow chart on the management of diabetic patients not requiring insulin and sent it to the 350 general practitioners in the Hunter Valley. The chart was explicit. It converted every GP to expert status in managing these patients without the need to read a book or attend a class. It was just a matter of the GP following the arrows from one situation to another. It was all there, even when to suspect pancreatic cancer—everything.

The flow chart soon spread beyond the Hunter Valley. In 1986, one pharmaceutical company, with my permission, printed hundreds of these charts and distributed them to GPs and hospitals throughout Australia; many were also distributed in India and Africa. I was informed in a letter from the company that an Indian doctor, when receiving a copy, stated that he had already seen my flow chart when visiting South Africa.

Dr W. Kalk, principal physician, University of Witwatersrand, South Africa, wrote to me on 11 January 1983 requesting a copy of my flow chart and stating, "My plan is to try and educate General Practitioners through our University Department etc. A simple flow chart would help us a great deal." I sent him the flow chart.

In 1985, Dr Julio Freijanes, Hospital Nacional, "Marques De Valdecilla," Santander, Spain wrote: "I would appreciate all information you can send us on your programs of patient education and postgraduate training for medical and nursing staff etc."

Many others wrote or were observers at our education courses. The world was, and always will be, full of doctors and other health professionals endeavouring to improve the lives of their fellow citizens.

A patient record card was produced. All patients carried one as their health record and presented it to every doctor or allied health professional they visited. Each professional recorded relevant facts and read the other recorded facts, and so all were informed of the others' actions without the laborious and inefficient chore of letter-writing to multiple recipients. This card was subsequently copied elsewhere in Australia and overseas.

The national lay body, the Australian Diabetes Federation, and the Australian Diabetes Society (diabetes specialists and scientists) suggested the formation of the Diabetes Education Committee devoted to education of all Australian diabetics, and I was selected as chairman. Three dedicated nurses joined me: Jim Keane from Sydney, Helen Turley from Canberra, and Gwen Scott from Melbourne. We met each month in Newcastle to formulate plans to get essential information to as many Australian diabetics as possible. We produced a book, *Diabetes: Your Role in Its Control*, which went to reprint. Another achievement was, with the assistance of a dozen diabetes specialists, the production of *17 Important Points* which were, we all agreed, essential for every diabetic patient or carer to know. Having formulated this essential information, the problem was to find a method of getting it into the hands of all Australian diabetics, regardless of where they lived.

The solution was to write to and personally speak to the managing director of three pharmaceutical companies that provided medication and testing products used by diabetics. We requested that they change their product inserts to include *17 Important Points*. They agreed, and soon all patients in Australia and New Zealand, no matter the remoteness of their abode, were reading that essential advice about diabetes and its management. It was such a simple thing to do, but it brought vital education about diabetes to every diabetic person in Australia and New Zealand. It required the cooperation of a number of like-minded individuals plus the financial commitment of the pharmaceutical companies—the staff of which, I must tell you, are usually dedicated and have my admiration.

The major diabetic problem in Australia in 1985 was that there were an estimated 30,000 people with diabetes who were about to lose their eyesight. My original concern had been the few hundred of my patients in danger, but now the concern was for the 30,000. How could they be warned to have their eyes checked and laser given, if needed? It is important to point out that, at that time, very few doctors realised that older diabetic patients (type 2) were candidates for blindness, and so they were not referred to ophthalmologists for routine assessment. They were considered to have a mere "touch of sugar."

I produced in Newcastle a professional film, *A Touch of Sugar*, in which Paul Mitchell demonstrated the value of laser and the need for all diabetic people to have their eyes examined by an eye specialist. Money from the Lions Clubs of 201 N3 and the involvement of the Diabetic Retinopathy Subcommittee, of which I was convener, and of the Australian Diabetes Society were integral to the making of that twenty-four-minute documentary. Again, the goodwill of big business was required, and the film was shown on television on multiple occasions all over Australia as a free community service. On 30 January 1986, for example, twenty-four television channels throughout Australia showed this documentary. I received multiple written national and international compliments, including those from Switzerland and the Centers for Disease Control in the USA.

The above sad story of the complications suffered by many diabetic people prior to 1975 has now changed. Today a person with diabetes, having had ten, twenty, thirty, or forty years of correct insulin treatment, may be the healthiest and best citizen in any group. It must be acknowledged that these advances were only possible because of concurrent improvements in treatment. No education and stabilisation would have been successful without the invention of a small machine that each patient owned and used to measure the amount of sugar in the blood. An Australian, Stan Clarke, was at the forefront of this invention. The production of human insulin and its delivery in pens was crucial. The use of a laser to prevent blindness was another monumental advance during the "magic decade" in the management of diabetes, 1972–1982.

The people who listened and acted were crucial. Without Dr Elwin Currow's and Dr Jack Toohey's belief and support, the Diabetes Education and Stabilisation Centre would not have come into existence, and the other advances would not have followed. Professor Fred Hollows's involvement was of extreme importance, and his choice of Drs. Paul Mitchell and Paul Beaumont was crucial. But it was the dedication and belief of my colleagues and staff that made it happen.

Whilst I was undertaking my endeavours, there were others doing as much or more. Professor John Turtle was not only educating his diabetic clinic patients and diabetes educators from Australia and the Pacific but undertaking the complete training of NSW medical students.

Dr Martyn Sulway, also in Sydney, was very active and innovative in educating patients and allied health professionals. Exceedingly tall, he is a natural entertainer and was always a popular lecturer.

Dr Hal Breidahl had spent many years liaising with the Australian Diabetes Federation before the arrival on the Melbourne scene of the indomitable Dr Paul Zimmet. Paul thrived upon challenges and believed in being the best at whatever he was undertaking. In 1984, he commenced the International Diabetes Institute in Melbourne and made certain that the world knew that Australia existed.

Dr Pat Phillips of Adelaide was another pioneer who devoted his life to providing education and better management of diabetes, not only to his own patients but also to Australia as a whole.

Dr Tim Welbourne led us all in the epidemiology of diabetes, and Dr Alan Stocks was active in many fields in his home state of Queensland.

Tasmania's giant, Dr Gordon Senator, emulated Winston Churchill in all but physiognomy. I recall deciding against jumping from a seventeenth-floor hotel window in Adelaide when Senator's cigar smoke set the whole of the hotel's fire alarms into a frenzy. Panic stations, thanks to my friend Gordon Senator's cigar.

Dr Tony Stepanas cared for those in the ACT. Only the Northern

Territory lacked someone fighting for its diabetic population during the 1970s, but a remarkable man was watching from the wings. I write of Bill Raby, OBE, lawyer and ex-diplomat with no connection to medicine, but he had diabetes. Having spent a week as a patient at my diabetes centre, Bill was determined to obtain the same facilities in Darwin and was subsequently totally responsible for the NT government donating the funds for the NT's first diabetes centre. We helped a little when my team of doctors, nurses, podiatrist, and dieticians spent a week there holding demonstrations and lectures for professionals, patients, politicians, and press. The initial centre has gone from strength to strength throughout the Northern Territory and produces an excellent patient and doctor publication, *The Territory Way*.

It was mainly these people and me who were responsible for the introduction of patient education and management into Australia in the early and mid-1970s, but the concept was quickly adopted by other doctors, and diabetes education became widespread throughout our nation. There was such an increase in diabetes educators (nurses, dietitians, podiatrists, and others) that the Australian Diabetes Educators' Association was formed in 1981.

The concept of patient education then spread to other diseases and is now an essential part of the treatment of most medical conditions. All patient education, as an integral component of health, commenced with diabetes.

My rewards have been diverse. Firstly, I am grateful for being permitted to live long enough to see the diabetic teenagers of the 1970s being, forty years later, healthy, confident, and free of serious diabetic complications. Secondly, I am grateful for having been able to work with people who believed in what they were doing and enjoyed doing it. Thirdly, most of the patients were lovely people whom it was a pleasure and honour to meet and help. (It's true that I disliked some of the patients and, one way or another, moved them to another diabetologist's care.) In 1992, I was proud to receive Membership of the Order of Australia for "services to medicine and particularly diabetes education." Every member of my staff contributed to that service. I might have had more responsibility than the cook, but the cook was equally important.

Retirement from directorship of the Diabetes Education and

Stabilisation Centre in 1989 made it impossible for me to personally accept a Chinese diabetologist for training in 1993, so I referred his letter to others for action. I include his letter here, written twenty-one years after my initial basic lectures in Australia, as it confirms the worldwide recognition over those two decades of the personal and state need for patient education in the management of diabetes.

Dr Ru-gen Zhang
Department of Endocrinology and Metabolism
Shanghai Sixth Hospital
Shanghai 200233,
P. R. China
July,19,93.

Dear Professor Moffitt

I am an Attending physician working at the Department of Endocrinology and Metabolism, Shanghai Sixth People's Hospital, Shanghai Second Medical University and taking responsibility in diabetes education and clinical research in our department. With increased prevalence of diabetes in our country, diabetic complications gradually become one of the major health problems, so that diabetes education becomes more and more important in our country.

I still get IDF Short Training Fellowships from International Diabetes Federation and I think to get further training in diabetes education abroad with this Fellowships. Since you are the most distinguished diabetologist in the world and I am deeply impressed with your outstanding work in diabetes research and education. I write to you asking whether I can come to your hospital, learning the diabetes education and research in your hospital.

I should be most grateful if you could accept me and I will be very happy to receive your letter of agreement.

I am looking forward to hearing from you at your earliest convenience. Thank you.

Sincerely,
Ru-gen Zhang

Jose Marti, a nineteenth century Cuban, wrote, "It is better to build a fence around a cliff than a hospital below it." My contribution was a hundred years later, but better late than never.

Some Wry Observations

One of the joys of life is to observe something and then let one's imagination endeavour to explain the reason for what you have observed. I would like to share some of my mental perambulations with you. Please adopt the final one as a part of your own life.

Conversation with Jodie

It was early May, and the sun would set within the hour, as I raked the soil in which I would plant a clump of acacia on the morrow. It had been a good day and was made better by the sight of Jodie approaching along the gravel road from my neighbour's farm.

I had neither seen nor spoken to anybody for twenty-four hours, but even had I done so, I would have been delighted to see Jodie, and my voice was filled with happiness as I shouted a greeting. Jodie understood, and her pace quickened until soon she was licking my hand.

Jodie, you see, is an aged, arthritic, desexed, female cattle dog. She does not have any canine company, and she has no great expectations from life. It must have pleased her to hear, as she painfully walked the last fifty metres to my farm, the warmth in my voice.

Jodie's affectionate licking of my hand completed, I did a little dance as I promised her some meat and bones that were stored in an outside fridge, and she trotted beside me as I walked to it. Was it the food or my company she sought? Who cared! She was there, and we were both happy.

I watched her for some time, but bone chewing is not very entertaining, and I returned to my raking until a satiated Jodie joined me. That is when the conversation, which was not new to us, began. She stood about a metre from me and looked directly into my eyes as she barked. Barking is not a difficult language to learn, and I returned her message with the same sincerity as she had displayed and with our eyes locked. So there we were, a dog and an apparently normal human, taking turns to bark, one at the other. There was nothing else in the world but us at that moment.

After some time, Jodie left for home, possibly thinking, "He has a lot to learn about dog speak, but at least I have got someone to talk to."

When she was about a hundred metres away, I barked a final farewell—a serious mistake, as Jodie turned and commenced a slow return.

My God, what have I done? I thought and then quickly reached a solution and walked towards my house. Jodie turned towards her home.

She would return in three or four days and we would again speak of unknown things, each grateful to have someone who listened without interrupting.

Addendum

There has never been any doubt in my mind that Jodie was speaking directly to me and not just barking, and so I was pleased to read today that Hungarian scientists have demonstrated that dogs have voice areas in their brains in exactly the same areas as do humans. The lead author, Attila Andics, writing in *Current Biology*, said, "Now we can see the brain mechanisms so important to language are also there in dogs."

So I was not mad in believing that Jodie was trying to tell me something. Trust me. Your dog has a voice centre.

Seriously, why not try to have a barking conversation with your dog? Success won't happen overnight; it will require patience and a peaceful setting without distractions. Of course, if people get to know what you're doing, they will say that you are barking mad—and that I am as well.

This reminds me of an old pensioner patient of mine who lived in a shack in the middle of the bush many kilometres from neighbours. He was happy with his lot in life and fiercely independent. The birds, wallabies, and other fauna were the only company he needed. His particular friend, however, was a horse which lived in a paddock close to his house. He told me that each morning, upon arising, he would walk out onto the dirt in front of his shack and empty his bladder to the sound of a fond whinny from his horse. It was obvious to me that the greeting from his horse was important to him. Surely it cannot be that the whinny was just a noise—it must have been a spoken greeting. Methinks that time will show that horses also have voice areas in their brains, albeit not well developed.

That same patient surprised me when he told me of his reply to a priest who had had the temerity to criticise him for having lewd thoughts.

"And you would be better off helping poor people in Africa than sitting on your arse, getting fat in B—."

There was nothing wrong with my patient's voice centre.

Aural–Oral Synchronisation Syndrome

Humans and some other species have been endowed with special senses in the form of smell, sight, taste, and hearing, and I am sure that you are familiar with the basics of these senses. But you may not, indeed you could not, have heard of aural–oral synchronisation syndrome.

This is a common but previously unnamed condition, which you will recognize as I describe its features. It is my contribution to thinking, though I realise Gus Nossal would not agree with my mental perambulations.

Firstly, it is a condition in which the sufferers of the condition are not sufferers at all. They inflict the suffering upon the unfortunate accompanying persons: you and me.

People with this syndrome have a cochlear nerve (it carries sound from the ear to the brain) that becomes inactive when their vocal chords are immobile. This means that, when they stop speaking for even a split second, they become totally deaf—but hearing returns as soon as they resume speech. Put simply, the bearer of this condition can hear his or her voice but not yours.

Although the syndrome sufferers cannot hear others, any one of your words can trigger an overwhelming deluge of words, an avalanche of diction related or unrelated to your initiating words. Although incapable of hearing your words, the syndrome sufferer would be first in the queue if someone, ten metres away, whispered, "Free beer here."

After a great deal of thought, I have reached the unproven hypothesis that the bearers of this disease must have a neurological synapse capable of blocking selected transmissions along their cochlear nerves when their vocal cords are immobile. An anatomist I am not, and so the likelihood is remote of my anatomical prediction being fact, but as many of you will attest, the condition indisputably exists and therefore deserves a name.

It is because of the synergy between ear and voice that I have named the condition *aural–oral synchronisation syndrome*. Did I hear you say that your mother-in-law has it? Join the club.

The Pendulum

My knowledge of physics is rudimentary, and my knowledge of wind is small, but please permit me to tell you of an interesting observation I made concerning the action of wind when approaching an obstruction.

My new hay shed (the one described in the story about watermelons was blown over in a gale) has large doors on opposite sides so that trucks bringing or taking lucerne bales may enter on one side and leave on the other. One day, I was working about two metres inside the southern door through which blew a gentle southerly wind. As I worked, I noticed that between the door and me was a small piece of gravel suspended two centimetres above the floor by a single strand of spiderweb that originated from a beam five metres higher. The spiderweb pendulum was one metre closer to the door than I was.

To my surprise, I saw that the piece of gravel was not stationary but was frequently moving from left to right or right to left. I then realised that it changed its position in reverse to where I stood. If I moved one pace to the left, the gravel would go in the opposite direction; if I moved back to the right, the gravel would move again. In other words, the wind coming through the door towards me could sense me long before it reached me and change direction to pass on either my left- or right-hand side, and this change in direction of the wind was responsible for the changing position of the spiderweb pendulum.

Sometime later, I saw another spiderweb pendulum hanging motionless from a tree branch with the suspended piece of gravel one or two centimetres above the ground. I assume the explanation is that both spiders inadvertently landed upon a piece of gravel when lowering themselves from a much higher spot, and the spider having departed the scene, the single strand of web then contracted owing to evaporation and/ or elasticity, and the gravel was lifted off the ground.

Nothing marvellous, but it was interesting to have nature give me this private demonstration of wind action and pendulum production by spiders.

The demonstration of the main flow of a breeze being diverted prior to an obstruction makes me wonder whether I should, in future, stand in front of a brick wall during a gale, as the main force of the wind will have been diverted before reaching the wall and I might be standing comfortably and safely in relatively still air, whereas those people hiding on the lee side of the wall will be crushed if the wall is blown over. Just a thought.

And what advice would you give to the second horse in a paddock if, during a moderate wind, its companion already had its head against the lee of the sole tree? Where should the second horse stand? In front of the tree or behind the other horse, and in what direction should it face in either position? There are a number of imponderables, including the possibility that the head-on position behind the first horse may add an odoriferous second wind to the equation.

Commonsense

A London bobby Graham Furneaux dreamt, as he patrolled Grosvenor Square, of being an Australian boundary rider with his own horse and dog and he was welcomed with open arms when he arrived in the Snowy River Country. His life was blessed and in 1965 he was Senior Constable and the only policeman in charming, rugged Comboyne with Ellenborough Falls, the longest single drop waterfall in Australia, only a stone's throw from his home.

I was a house guest in 1965 with his wife Faye and sons Paul and Brad when Graham received a telephone call informing him that a young man was trapped under an overturned tractor and that a crane would be required to rescue him. Graham telephoned the local timber mill requesting that they send a mobile crane to the property that was about two kilometres away and I accompanied him as he picked up the bush-nurse with her kit including morphine and oxygen. The three of us were soon speeding on the twisting mountain road towards the accident.

"Slow down mate. The bloke will be dead and there is no point in us dying as well" was my unanswered request.

Shortly we turned through an open gate and below and around us was undulating green pasture with a small group of men and women standing beside a dry creek about a quarter of a kilometre from us. Upon arrival we were told that the young man was alive and so I took the morphine and oxygen before clambering down the creek bank and crawling into a narrow space beside the trapped man wedged between the overturned tractor and the diesel soaked earth. The victim was still in the driver's seat and facing upwards with one arm pinned to the ground by the mudguard of the tractor and one leg was held tightly over his abdomen, chest and shoulder by the tractor so he either had a fractured or dislocated hip joint. He was alive because the right hand wheel of the tractor was resting upon the 25cm high left hand corner of the dray that he had been pulling up the steep bank of the creek. The dray had saved his life.

We talked as I gave the morphine and oxygen before assessing the situation and thinking about his rescue. How could we get the tractor off him without it moving and crushing him was my first thought. It was presently stable but any attempt to lift the tractor by a rope or chain attached to a crane would dislodge its right wheel from the crucial support of the dray with a resultant collapse of the tractor onto the man.

More vehicles arrived with some carrying timber workers and they also understandably made a decision to obtain the mobile crane from the timber mill at Comboyne. From under the tractor I told them that the only safe and simple method of saving the man was to dig a narrow trench under the tractor and the man would fall into the trench. Unfortunately none of the group had a shovel.

Mobile phones being in the future, Grahame drove back to the police station, telephoned an ambulance and then a number of people whom he reasoned would own a shovel. So the man was rescued with a dislocated hip as his only serious injury.

This story has two messages. The first is that the obvious solution is not always the correct one so stop and think. The second is that the towing point of a towing vehicle such as a tractor or quad bike must never be higher than the towing point of the object being towed. Beware ascending slopes.

Moffitt's Foxhole Test

Perhaps you may care to know of a test that I use when needed. This test could save you from a number of serious losses. The test is simple. It is a test of another person's character, not your bravery.

I apply it to people who ask me to lend them money or lend my name to some petition or other in which I could be left holding the bag. You will find a multitude of situations where you will receive good guidance in making a decision if you apply my Foxhole Test first.

For example, your sister's new boyfriend asks you to guarantee his bank loan so that he can start a business. If he fails the Foxhole Test, find an excuse to avoid risking your money.

Your workmate Tom's nice-looking yacht has a broken rudder, and he can't take the money from his term deposit, as he will lose all the accumulated bank interest. Could you lend him $1,500 for two months? Apply my test and think hard.

What is the Foxhole Test? I picture myself in a small foxhole surrounded on all sides by baddies intent upon killing me. Fortunately, I have help in the form of a person who is in the foxhole with me. Both of us will survive as long as each protects the other's back. But there is an important addition to the foxhole: it has an escape trench and the other person could slip down the trench to safety, leaving me (or you, if you are applying my test to someone) to be shot in the back.

So all you have to do is ask yourself if the person who is asking you for money, support, or whatever would slip quietly down the escape trench when the going gets tough. If the answer is yes, then bow out of the request no matter how much you may be hated.

Just for fun, start secretly using my Foxhole Test upon people whom you know or work with, and you may get some surprises about their character. Always use it where money or your name is at stake. Start with your boss and pray that he or she passes the test.

Adieu.

Printed in the United States
By Bookmasters